Handwriting 3

FOR YOUNG CATHOLICS

WRITTEN BY
SETON STAFF

SETON PRESS
FRONT ROYAL, VA

Executive Editor: Dr. Mary Kay Clark
Editors: Seton Staff

Seton Home Study School
1350 Progress Drive
Front Royal, VA 22630
540-636-9990
540-636-1602 fax

For more information, visit us on the Web at www.setonhome.org.
Contact us by e-mail at info@setonhome.org.

ISBN: 978-1-60704-067-5

Cover: *Pope St. Gregory the Great Writing his Gospel Homilies*, Carlo Saraceni

DEDICATED TO THE SACRED HEART OF JESUS

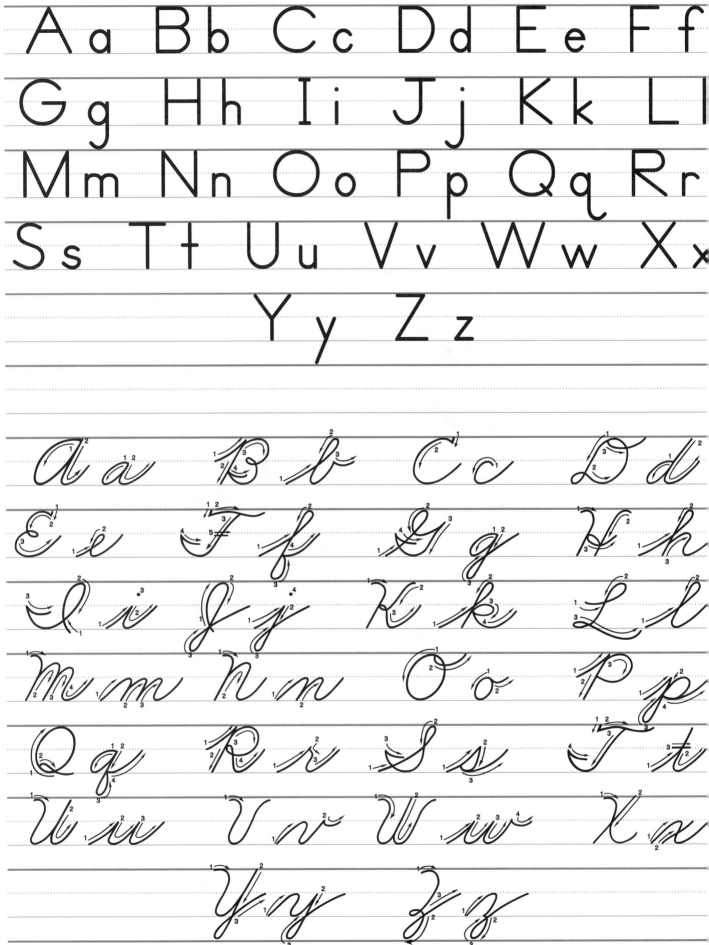

Table of Contents

Fourth Quarter

Week

Correct Writing Position

Left-Handed - Manuscript

Right-Handed - Manuscript

Left-Handed - Cursive

Right-Handed - Cursive

Introduction for Parents

Welcome to Handwriting 3! You will notice that the handwriting style in this book is based on Zaner-Bloser's new simplified handwriting style. The computer age has affected handwriting, as people have demanded a more simple handwriting style rather than the elaborate beautiful handwriting with flourishes and loops.

The purpose of this Third Grade handwriting book is to help your child refine his handwriting skills in both the manuscript printing and the cursive letters. Both are important in the demands of our modern lives.

A secondary purpose of this handwriting book is to give your child an appreciation of our Catholic Faith by including beautiful religious art and words, phrases, and sentences that relate to our Faith. What we write can strengthen our faith and the faith of others. In fact, we give honor and glory to God through our concern for others by writing legibly. The reader should not need to struggle to try to read our handwriting.

For your own reference, you might like to know that our Kindergarten handwriting book teaches lowercase manuscript (or printing), the First Grade book teaches lowercase and uppercase manuscript handwriting, and the Second Grade handwriting book focuses on lowercase cursive letters. In this book, you will find plenty of opportunities for review of manuscript handwriting, as well as cursive, but the emphasis will be on learning uppercase cursive letters.

One page in the front of the book displays each manuscript letter and each cursive letter, with arrows directing how to write the letter. As you go through the lessons, you will see these letters with arrows printed on the practice pages. You will notice that some letters with arrows tend to be more slanted, and with a longer sweep than the letters for tracing. We were not able to find letter fonts with the arrows that were exactly the same as the letters in the simplified practice lessons. However, they are so close that the tiny difference should not be a problem.

The letters are presented in the practice lessons in order, according to similar strokes. The letters are shaded so that they can be easily traced over with a pencil or a pen. The words and sentences are shaded also. After tracing the letters, words, or sentences, the student should be able to write them freely.

You will notice that we have an Appendix at the back of this book. These are extra drill pages for each manuscript letter, both small and capital.

Seton's SEM department sells blank handwriting tablets. Enrolled students receive a tablet. If you decide to order more, or if you are not enrolled and need a tablet, be sure to order the correct grade level, because the height of the space for the letters differs for each grade.

Enrolled students also receive daily lesson plans, which include readiness activities and more detailed instructions for strokes, as well as extra drill pages that can be downloaded from the Seton website.

Encourage your child to develop his handwriting skills by using his best handwriting in the other schoolwork. By the end of this school year, your child should be proficient in the art of handwriting. With the use of computers, many children are not learning how to write legibly. We need to explain to our children that there are still situations in life when good handwriting is necessary or appropriate. For instance, if a child is sending a birthday greeting or letter to his grandmother, it should be personal and written by hand; a personal handwritten note sends a message of caring and love.

Good, legible penmanship conveys a personal concern for the reader. We hope that beautiful handwriting, even if simplified, will return to our country, along with a return of Christian culture. God bless you and your family as you teach your children how to express themselves in good handwriting.

Adoration of the Magi

Prayer
by Hilaire Belloc

Jesus Christ,
Thou Child so wise,
Bless mine hands
And fill mine eyes,
And bring my soul
To Paradise.

Print the poem "Prayer" in your best manuscript.

Study the manuscript letter alongside each of the cursive letters and numerals.

a *a*   b *b*   c *c*   d *d*

e *e*   f *f*   g *g*   h *h*

i *i*   j *j*   k *k*   l *l*

m *m*   n *n*   o *o*   p *p*

q *q*   r *r*   s *s*   t *t*

u *u*   v *v*   w *w*   x *x*

y *y*   z *z*

1 2 3 4 5 6 7 8 9 0

penmanship *penmanship*

church *church*

homeschool *homeschool*

rosary *rosary*

Study the manuscript letter alongside each uppercase cursive letter.

A A B B C C D D
E E F F G G H H
I I J J K K L L
M M N N O O P P
Q Q R R S S T T
U U V V W W X X
Y Y Z Z

Print the words in manuscript below each sentence.

Mary is the Mother of Jesus.

Jesus Christ is God.

Can you read this manuscript?
Trace and print the words in manuscript below each line.

Dear Lord,

Make my heartbeats

A prayer and song

To honor and praise You

All the night long.

Trace and print the words in manuscript below each line.

You hid Yourself, Dear Lord,

as other children do;

But oh, how great

was their reward

Who sought three days

for You!

Finding of the Child Jesus in the Temple

Important Strokes

Undercurve Stroke

Trace and copy these undercurve strokes.

Downcurve Stroke

Trace and copy these downcurve strokes.

Overcurve Stroke

Trace and copy these overcurve strokes.

Slant Stroke

Trace and copy these slantcurve strokes.

Trace and print the lowercase cursive alphabet in manuscript.

a b c d e f g

h i j k l m n

o p q r s t u

v w x y z

Trace and print these cursive words in manuscript.

be is to up

on no my it

St. Agnes of Montepulciano saw Our Lady many times when she was praying.

is him write

is him write

Trace and copy.

i i i i i i

i i i i i i

Join the cursive i. Trace and copy.

ii ii ii ii ii

ii ii ii ii ii

tot tiny telephone

tot tiny telephone

Trace and copy.

t t t t t t t

t t t t t t t t

Trace and copy.

tt tt tt tt tt tt

ti ti ti ti ti ti

it it it it it it

us unite you

us unite you

Trace and copy.

Trace and copy.

17

4-1

W w̃ẃ̃

will water was

will water was

Trace and copy.

w w w w w w

w w w w w w

Trace and copy.

wi wi iw iw

ww uw wt ww

wit wit wit

Let's review what we've learned.

Trace and copy.

it ti iti it tu tiu

tui itu wi tu iuw

tiw wt wut wit wu

tut wit wut tuw

tutu tuti wuti

St. Rose of Lima

rose are rainbow

rose are rainbow

Trace and copy.

r r r r r r

ri ru rit write ur

seven sin sick

seven sin sick

Trace and copy.

s s s s s s s

sit its wrist is suit

pray paint sup

pray   paint   sup

Trace and copy.

p p p p p p p p

pit purr pups sip

just jump jars

just   jump   jars

Trace and copy.

j j j j j j j j

ij puj wuj jut just

Let's review what we've learned.

Trace and copy.

pr sp rs ju pi it is

rip trip tip sup writ

rust trust just turist

rusts turists wrist jut

sups suit tuss wrists

a | *a*

aunt apples art

aunt apples art

Trace and copy.

a a a a a a a a a

air war start watt

c | *c*

carve carriage can

carve carriage can

Trace and copy.

c c c c c c c c c

carts circus pact

quart quick queen

quart quick queen

Trace and copy.

q q q q q q q q

quail square quart

good give grows

good give grows

Trace and copy.

g g g g g g g g

gust green gas germ

St. Dominic with Pope Honorius

d *d*

deer dentist dry

deer dentist dry

Trace and copy.

d d d d d d d d

draw dust dip aid

o *o*

open pope tool

open pope tool

Trace and copy.

o o o o o o o o

poor doors oat out

27

Let's review what we've learned.

Trace and copy.

drop quart grow dart

door card ajar post

squirt cactus upstairs

jars coast goat goad

carrot stops roost

6-2

n ℳ

nine nickel new

nine nickel new

Trace and copy.

m m m m m m m m m m

saint song marrow

m ℳ

many mortal

many mortal

Trace and copy.

m m m m m m m m m m

man woman mind

St. Thomas Aquinas, the "Dumb Ox"

virtue   vocation

virtue   vocation

Trace and copy.

vain visit vacation

boxes fox oxen fix

boxes fox oxen fix

Trace and copy.

tax mix taxi mixing

yes story yellow

yes story yellow

Trace and copy.

y y y y y y y y

yours dairy stay pity

zebra zipper zero

zebra zipper zero

Trace and copy.

z z z z z z z z

zoo zigzag dizzy quiz

Let's review what we've learned.

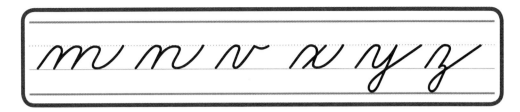

Trace and copy.

jazzy mix zip quiz

cozy toy very now

yes yen many jazzy

music gravy nanny

zoom vast morning

33

7-2

love holy life

love holy life

Trace and copy.

l l l l l l l l l l

llama loss quilt ill

grace eager edge

grace eager edge

Trace and copy.

e e e e e e e e

eggs event every eels

kangaroos kayak

kangaroos   kayak

Trace and copy.

k k k k k k k k k k

kite kiss kilts quick

thy heaven holy

thy   heaven   holy

Trace and copy.

h h h h h h h h h h

church heart honor

The Baptism of St. Dominic

baptize birth obey

baptize birth obey

Trace and copy.

b b b b b b b b

bigger habit boxes bye

feast fast find

feast fast find

Trace and copy.

f f f f f f f f

fever fancy gruff of

37

8-1

Let's review what we've learned.

Trace and copy.

beef heel kick fish if

look baby king bell

finish host foe holier

lunch kilo beak high

believe enough baptize

Learning Something New

Uppercase or Capital Letters

Trace.

May all I think or
say or do
Be done, dear God for
you.
Always be good and
do your best
Then trust in God to
do the rest.

Now go back and circle all the uppercase, or capital, letters.

The Uppercase Alphabet

Uppercase, or capital, letters begin a name or start a sentence.
All uppercase letters are tall letters. Trace and copy.

A *B* *C*

Say each uppercase letter aloud.
Circle the letters that start your first, middle, and last names.

A B C D E F G

H I J K L M N

O P Q R S T U

V W X Y Z

The part of a letter that goes down below the baseline is called its descende
 Underline the three uppercase letters that have a descender.

Father Perez urges Queen Isabel to give Columbus ships.

Madonna and Child with the Angels

Let's Match the Alphabet

Draw a line from the uppercase letter to the same one in manuscript. Use a ruler to draw your line.

Touch the headline. Curve left and down to the baseline; curve under and up to the headline. Pause; slant left to the baseline; curve under and up to the midline.

Touch the midline. Curve left and down to the baseline. Curve under and up to the midline. Pause; slant left to the baseline; curve under and up to the midline.

A a

Adam Anne Able
Adam   Anne   Able

Trace and copy.

a a a a a a a a

Trace and copy.

Alex Advent America

Arthur Alice Ascension

Are you going to be

an American artist?

45

9-2

Touch the headline. Short slant down; pause; curve left and down to the baseline; curve under and up to the midline.

Touch the below the midline. Curve up to the midline; curve left and down to the baseline; curve under and up to the midline.

C C

Christ Church Chant

Christ Church Chant

Trace and copy.

C C C C C C C C C

Trace and copy.

Christopher Columbus

Christ Catholic Christmas

Carl came to Canada

in a car.

Touch the headline. Curve left and down to the baseline; curve under and up to the headline. Loop down slightly; curve right to the headline.

Touch the midline. Curve left and down to the baseline; curve under and up to the midline. Pause; check stroke.

48

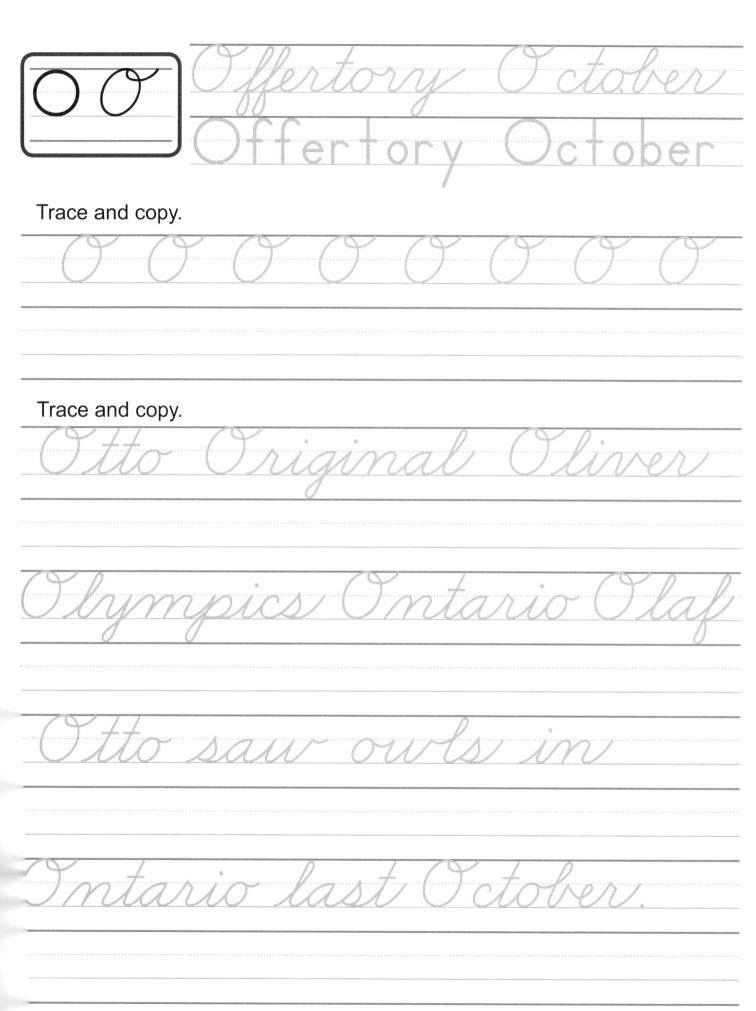

Offertory October
Offertory October

Trace and copy.

O O O O O O O O O

Trace and copy.

Otto Original Oliver

Olympics Ontario Olaf

Otto saw owls in

Ontario last October.

Touch the headline. Short slant down. Pause; curve left and down looping around the midline; curve left and down to the baseline, making the bottom loop larger; curve under and up.

Touch the baseline. Curve under and up to the midline. Loop back; slant left to the baseline, making a loop. Curve under and up to the midline.

E E

Eve England Easter
Eve England Easter

Trace and copy.

E   E   E   E   E   E   E   E

Trace and copy.

Edward Elizabeth Erin

Easter Esther Epiphany

Easter and Epiphany

are Catholic feasts.

51

Let's review what we've learned.

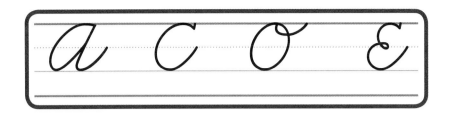

Trace and copy.

Adam and Eve Advent

Arctic Ocean Atlantic

Christmas and Easter

Christ Christian Chant

Ohio Eternity Ottawa

Notre Dame Cathedral, Ottawa, Canada

Touch just below the headline. Curve forward; slant left to the baseline. Pause; curve up to below the headline; slant left to the baseline. Pause; curve up to below the headline; slant left to the baseline; curve under and up.

Touch the baseline. Curve up to the midline; slant left to the baseline. Pause; curve up to the midline; slant left to the baseline. Pause; curve up to the midline; slant left to the baseline; curve under and up.

Michael Missouri

Michael Missouri

Trace and copy.

m m m m m m m m m

Trace and copy.

Mass Mary Monday

March May Michigan

Mother Mary gave us

the Miraculous Medal.

Touch just below the headline. Curve forward; slant left to the baseline. Pause; curve up and right below the headline; slant left to the baseline; curve under and up to the midline.

Touch the baseline. Curve up and right to the midline; slant left to the baseline. Pause; curve up and right to the midline; slant left to the baseline; curve under and up to the midline.

Nicene Nazareth Noe

Nicene Nazareth Noe

Trace and copy.

n n n n n n n n n

Trace and copy.

November Nina Nevada

Nancy Naples Nativity

At Mass, we say the

Nicene Creed.

Touch just below the headline. Curve forward; slant left to the baseline. Lift. Touch just below the headline; curve back; slant left to the baseline. Retrace; loop at the midline; curve right to the midline.

Touch the baseline. Curve under and up to the headline. Loop back; slant left to the baseline. Curve up to the midline; slant left to the baseline, keeping the slant strokes parallel. Curve under and up.

Heaven Holy Hour
Heaven Holy Hour

Trace and copy.

H H H H H H H H H

Trace and copy.

Heaven Hell Holy Hour

Helen Host Hawaii

Holy Communion is

the key to Heaven.

11-1

Touch just below the headline. Curve forward; slant left to the baseline. Lift. Double-curve down to the midline. Curve forward and down; curve under and up to the midline.

Touch the baseline. Curve under and up to the headline. Loop back; slant left to the baseline. Curve up to the midline; curve forward; curve under. Pause; slant right to the baseline; curve under and up.

K K

Kingdom   Kansas
Kingdom   Kansas

Trace and copy.

K   K   K   K   K   K   K   K

Trace and copy.

King   Kentucky   Kim

Kind   Kenneth   Kennel

Christ is King of

Heaven and Earth.

61   11-2

Holy Mass

Let's review what we've learned.

Trace and copy.

Maryland Matrimony

New England Kentucky

New Hampshire Noah

North Korea Holy Mass

Host Kingdom Heaven

Touch just below the headline. Curve forward; slant left to the baseline; curve under and up; curve up and right to the headline.

Touch the baseline. Curve up and over to the midline; slant left to the baseline; curve under and up to the midline. Check stroke.

Veronica's Veil
Veronica's Veil

Trace and copy.

V V V V V V V V V V

Trace and copy.

Vespers Virginia Victor

Vatican Valentine

Veronica's Veil is a

relic of the Vatican.

Touch just below the headline. Curve forward; slant left to the baseline; curve under and up to the headline. Pause; slant left to the baseline; curve under and up to the midline.

Touch the baseline. Curve under and up to the midline. Pause; slant left to the baseline. Curve under and up to the midline. Pause; slant left to the baseline. Curve under and up to the midline.

66

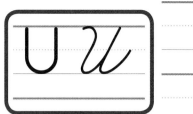

Ursula   Unction

Ursula   Unction

Trace and copy.

U U U U U U U U

Trace and copy.

Ursula Unction Utah

Uranus   Ursuline

Ursula is the model

for the Ursuline nuns.

Touch just below the headline. Curve forward; slant left to the baseline; curve under and up to the headline. Pause; slant left through the baseline. Loop back, curve up to the midline, crossing the loop near the baseline.

Touch the baseline. Curve up and right to the midline. Slant left to the baseline; curve under and up to the midline. Pause; slant left through the baseline. Loop back; curve up, crossing the loop near the baseline.

Y y

York Yolanda
York Yolanda

Trace and copy.

Y Y Y Y Y Y Y Y Y Y

Trace and copy.

York Yolanda Yves

Yukon Yemen Yalta

New York was one of

the original colonies.

69

12-2

Touch just below the headline. Curve forward and down to the baseline. Curve up slightly, right, and down through the baseline. Loop. Curve up to the midline, crossing the loop near the baseline.

Touch the baseline. Curve up and over to the midline; slant left to the baseline. Loop down through the baseline; curve back and up to the midline, crossing the loop near the baseline.

Z z

Zita Zealot

Zita Zealot

Trace and copy.

Z Z Z Z Z Z Z Z

Trace and copy.

Zachary Zebedee Zoe

Zurich Zanzibar Zita

Zachary was visited

by an angel.

St. Peter's, Vatican City

Let's review what we've learned.

Trace and copy.

Virgin Mary Yvonne

Extreme Unction A to Z

Vulgate Yule Virgil

Zacharias the prophet

Urban the pope

Touch just below the headline. Curve forward; slant left to the baseline; curve under and up to the headline. Pause; slant left to the baseline; curve under and up; curve right to the headline.

Touch the baseline. Curve under and up to the midline. Pause; slant left to the baseline. Curve under and up to the midline. Pause; slant left to the baseline. Curve under and up to the midline. Pause; check stroke.

W W

Wednesday Word

Wednesday Word

Trace and copy.

W W W W W W W W W

Trace and copy.

William Wales Word

Wednesday Wyoming

William of York is

an English saint.

Touch just below the headline. Curve forward; slant left slightly to the baseline; curve under and up. Lift. Touch the headline; slant left to the baseline, crossing near the midline.

Touch the baseline. Curve up and over to the midline; slant left slightly to the baseline; curve under and up to the midline. Lift. Touch the midline; slant left to the baseline.

76

X X

Xavier   X-ray
Xavier   X-ray

Trace and copy.

X X X X X X X X X X

Trace and copy.

Xavier   Xavierian

X-ray   Xenon

Xavier is a name

that means "savior."

Let's review what we've learned.

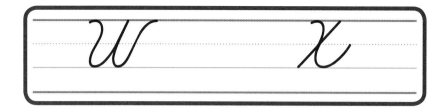

Trace and copy.

Whitsunday Worship

Xavier X-ray Xenon

Way of the Cross

Holy Water Wisdom

Washington Walter

St. Francis Xavier baptizes an Oriental queen.

Touch the headline. Slant left slightly; curve forward and right to the headline; lift. Double-curve down to the baseline, curve up and left to the midline. Retrace, curve right.

Touch the baseline. Curve under and up to the headline. Pause; slant left to the baseline. Pause; curve under and up to the midline. Lift. Slide right above the midline.

T J

Thomas Tuesday
Thomas Tuesday

Trace and copy.

T T T T T T T T

Trace and copy.

Trinity Thursday

Toledo Thailand

The "Tantum Ergo" is

by Thomas Aquinas.

Touch the headline. Slant left slightly. Curve forward to the headline; lift. Double-curve down to the baseline, curve back to the midline. Pause; retrace, curve right. Lift. Touch the midline, slide right.

Touch the baseline. Curve under and up to the headline. Loop back; slant left through the baseline. Loop forward and up, closing the loop near the baseline. Curve under and up.

F F

February Faith

February Faith

Trace and copy.

F F F F F F F F

Trace and copy.

Fatima First Friday

Father Francis Faith

Many Catholics eat

fish on Fridays.

Touch just below the baseline. Curve up and left to the headline; slant left through the baseline. Loop back; curve up to the midline, crossing the loop near the baseline.

Touch the baseline. Curve under and up to the midline. Pause; slant left through the baseline. Loop back; curve up and right to the midline, closing the loop near the baseline. Lift. Dot.

J J

Jesus January

Jesus January

Trace and copy.

J J J J J J J J J J

Trace and copy.

Jesus John Job Jacinta

Jewish Jamaica Jericho

Sacred Heart of Jesus,

have mercy on us!

Touch just below the baseline. Curve up and left to the headline; curve down and up to the midline. Pause; retrace; curve right.

Touch the baseline. Curve under and up to the midline. Pause; slant left to the baseline. Pause; curve under and up to the midline. Lift. Dot above the midline.

Indian   Iowa

Indian   *Iowa*

Trace and copy.

I I I I I I I I I I

Trace and copy.

Ingrid Icon India

Ignatius   Illinois

Isaac Jogues was

martyred by Iroquois.

Touch the baseline. Curve back, up and right to the headline; curve down to the baseline; retrace; curve forward; curve under, ending below the baseline.

Touch the midline. Curve left and down to the baseline. Curve under and up to the midline. Pause; slant left through the baseline; loop forward, closing the loop near the baseline. Curve under and up.

Q Q

Queen   Quebec
Queen   Quebec

Trace and copy.

Q Q Q Q Q Q Q Q

Trace and copy.

Queen   Queenship

Quebec Quentin Quito

The Queenship of

Mary is a feast day.

Let's review what we've learned.

Trace and copy.

The Immaculate Heart

Franciscan Friars

Jesus, Mary, Joseph

Queen of Heaven

Isaac Jogues Indians

15-1

Jesus, Mary, and Joseph flee into Egypt.

Touch the baseline. Curve under and up to the headline; loop back, closing the loop near the midline, curve down to the baseline, and back to the midline. Pause, retrace, curve right.

Touch the baseline. Curve under and up to the midline. Retrace; curve down to the baseline and back. Curve under, touching the baseline, and up to the midline.

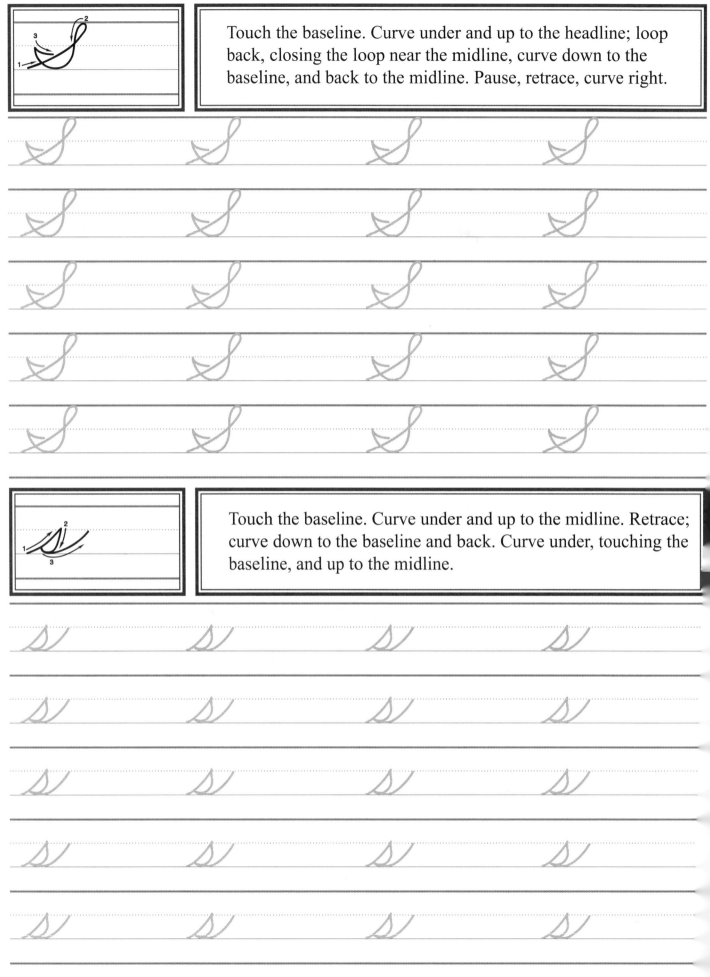

Sacred Scripture
Sacred Scripture

Trace and copy.

S S S S S S S S S S

Trace and copy.

Saturday Sunday

September Sacrament

Saint Stephen of

Hungary was a king.

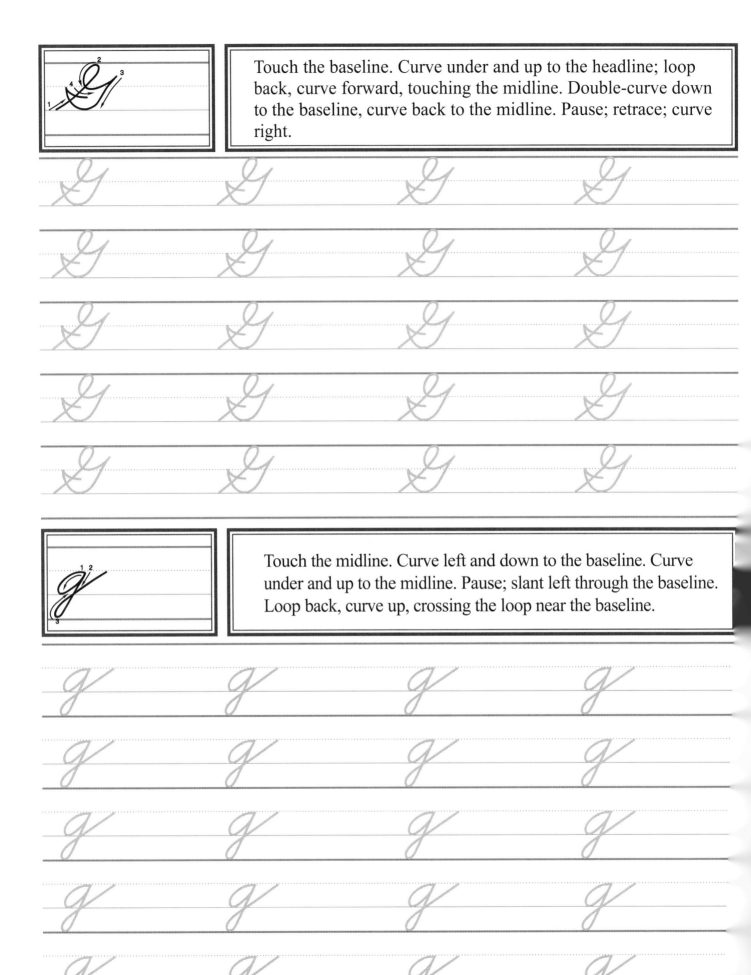

Touch the baseline. Curve under and up to the headline; loop back, curve forward, touching the midline. Double-curve down to the baseline, curve back to the midline. Pause; retrace; curve right.

Touch the midline. Curve left and down to the baseline. Curve under and up to the midline. Pause; slant left through the baseline. Loop back, curve up, crossing the loop near the baseline.

God Glory Grace

Trace and copy.

G G G G G G G G

Trace and copy.

German George Grace

Gulf Gabriel Gregorian

The Glorious Mysteries

Gregory the Great

Touch the headline. Curve left and down, resting the loop on the baseline; curve down to the baseline and up to the headline, loop down slightly, curve right and up to the headline.

Touch the midline. Curve left and down to the baseline. Curve under and up to the headline. Pause; slant left to the baseline; curve under and up to the midline.

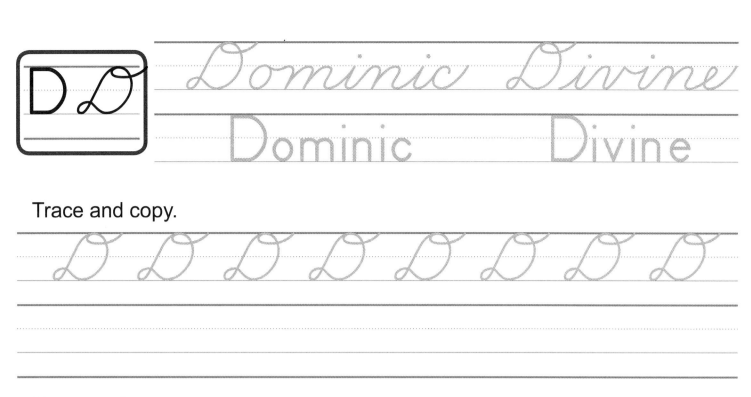

D D

Dominic Divine

Dominic Divine

Trace and copy.

D D D D D D D D

Trace and copy.

December Dominican

Diana David Daniel

David, the shepherd

boy, slew Goliath.

15-4

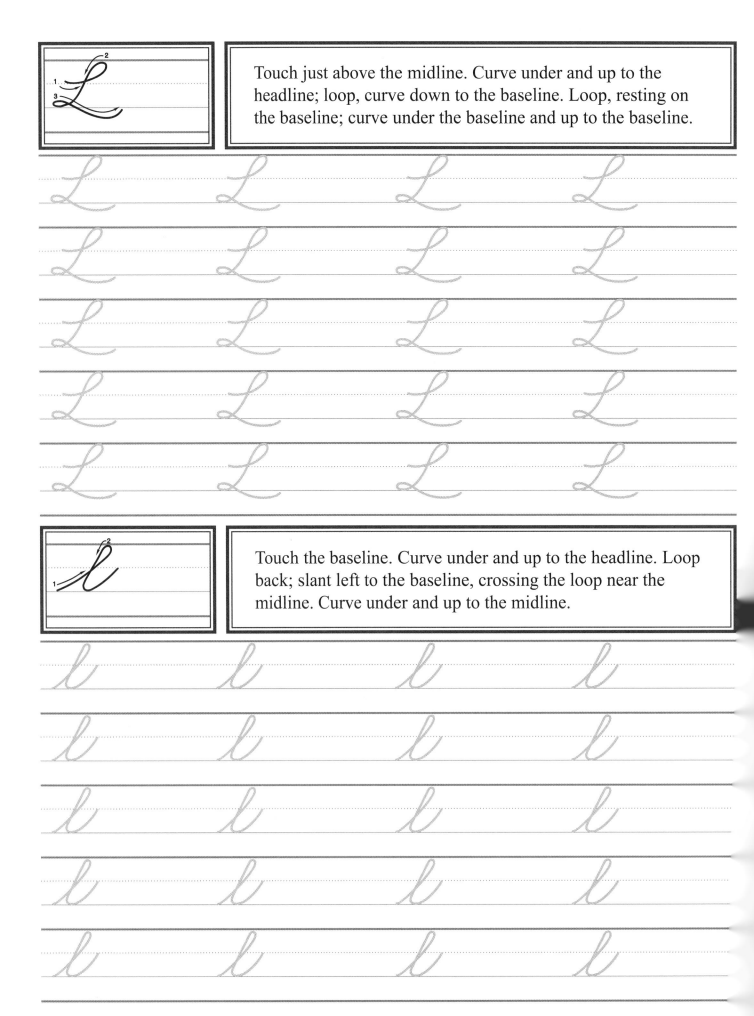

Touch just above the midline. Curve under and up to the headline; loop, curve down to the baseline. Loop, resting on the baseline; curve under the baseline and up to the baseline.

Touch the baseline. Curve under and up to the headline. Loop back; slant left to the baseline, crossing the loop near the midline. Curve under and up to the midline.

L L

St. Louis   Lady

St. Louis   Lady

Trace and copy.

L L L L L L L L L L

Trace and copy.

Lucy Lincoln Louis

Limbo London Lima

Our Lady loves us.

St. Lucy, pray for us.

99

The Angel Gabriel asks Mary to be the Mother of Jesus.

100

Let's review what we've learned.

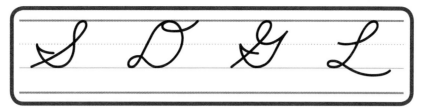

Trace and copy.

Glory to God   Gabriel

Dante Divine Dallas

Grace and Love of God

Saint Laurence

Last Supper

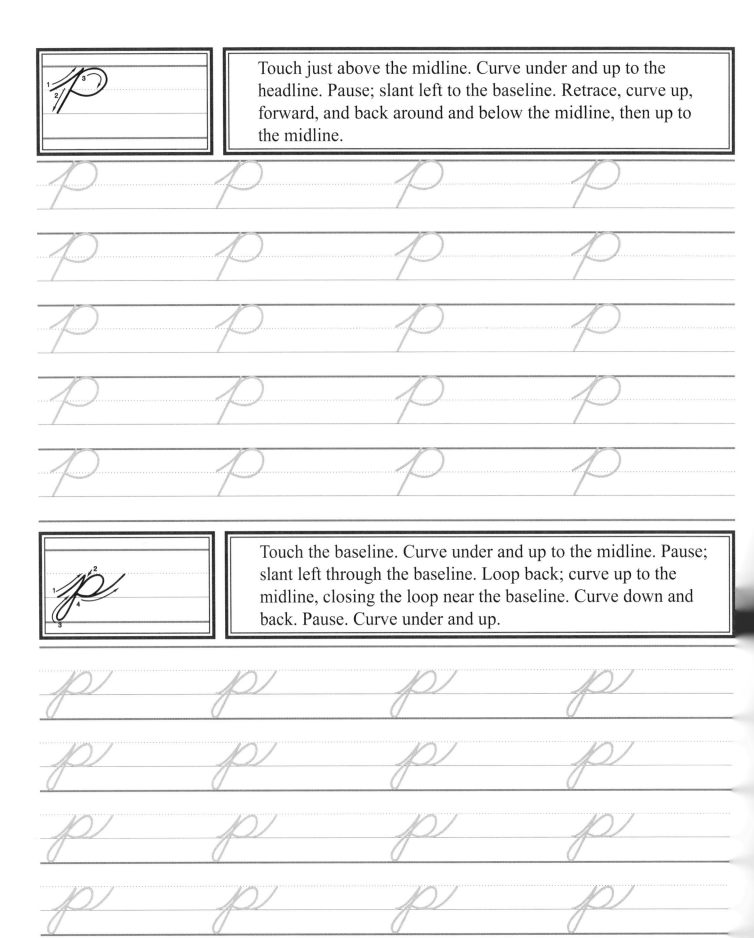

Touch just above the midline. Curve under and up to the headline. Pause; slant left to the baseline. Retrace, curve up, forward, and back around and below the midline, then up to the midline.

Touch the baseline. Curve under and up to the midline. Pause; slant left through the baseline. Loop back; curve up to the midline, closing the loop near the baseline. Curve down and back. Pause. Curve under and up.

P P

Penance Pentecost
Penance   Purgatory

Trace and copy.

P P P P P P P P P

Trace and copy.

Paul Peter Purgatory

Penance Pope Paris

Jesus Christ made St.

Peter the first pope.

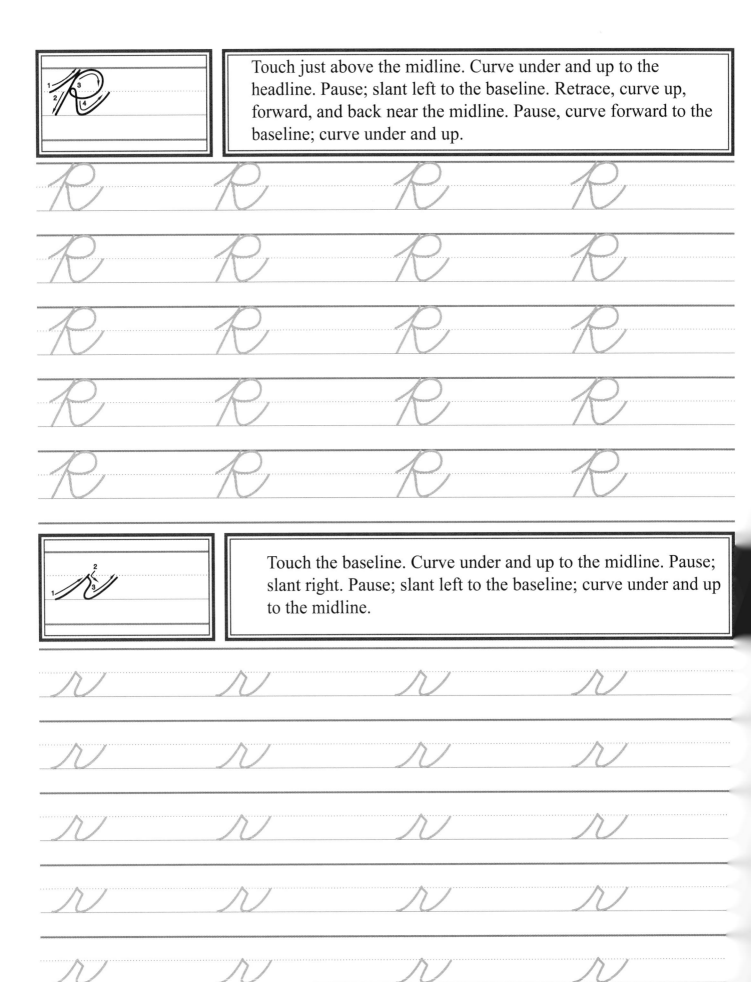

Touch just above the midline. Curve under and up to the headline. Pause; slant left to the baseline. Retrace, curve up, forward, and back near the midline. Pause, curve forward to the baseline; curve under and up.

Touch the baseline. Curve under and up to the midline. Pause; slant right. Pause; slant left to the baseline; curve under and up to the midline.

Regina   Raphael

Regina   Raphael

Trace and copy.

R R R R R R R R R R

Trace and copy.

Rosary Rome Richard

Rose   Requiem   Rita

Raphael showed Tobias

how to catch the fish.

Touch just above the midline. Curve under and up to the headline. Pause; slant left to the baseline. Retrace; curve up, and forward; loop around the midline, curve forward, down, and back, touching the slant stroke. Curve right.

Touch the baseline. Curve under and up to the headline. Loop back; slant left to the baseline, crossing the loop near the midline. Curve under and up to the midline. Pause; check stroke.

B B

Bible Benediction

Bible   Benediction

Trace and copy.

B B B B B B B B B

Trace and copy.

Blessed Brazil Bishop

Boston Baptism Bible

Baptism makes me

an heir to Heaven.

Let's review what we've learned.

Trace and copy.

Byzantine Rite Roman

The Real Presence

Holy Body and Blood

Potomac River Penance

Blessed Bruna Pellesi

The Blessed Virgin Mary intercedes for the souls in Purgatory.

Let's Review All the Uppercase Letters

Copy the uppercase letters on the lines below.Use your best cursive.

A C O

E M N

H K V U

Y Z W X

T F I

L Q S

G D L

P R B

Now write your full name in your best cursive handwriting.

Write the uppercase cursive letters for the manuscript ones.

A C O E

M N H K V

U Y Z W

X T F J I

Q S G D

L P R B

Write these phrases in cursive.

United States of America

John Paul Jones

Gate of Heaven

Write the cursive uppercase letters in Alphabet order.

Write the words and phrases in cursive.

Roman Catholic Church

Apostles' Creed

Holy Day of Obligation

Rhyme Time

Using your best cursive, write each line of the poem below.

We love Our Lady dearly.

Her words we must obey:

"Do reparation for your sins.

Pray the Rosary every day."

Write your name and address on the lines below.

Name:

Address:

City, state, zip:

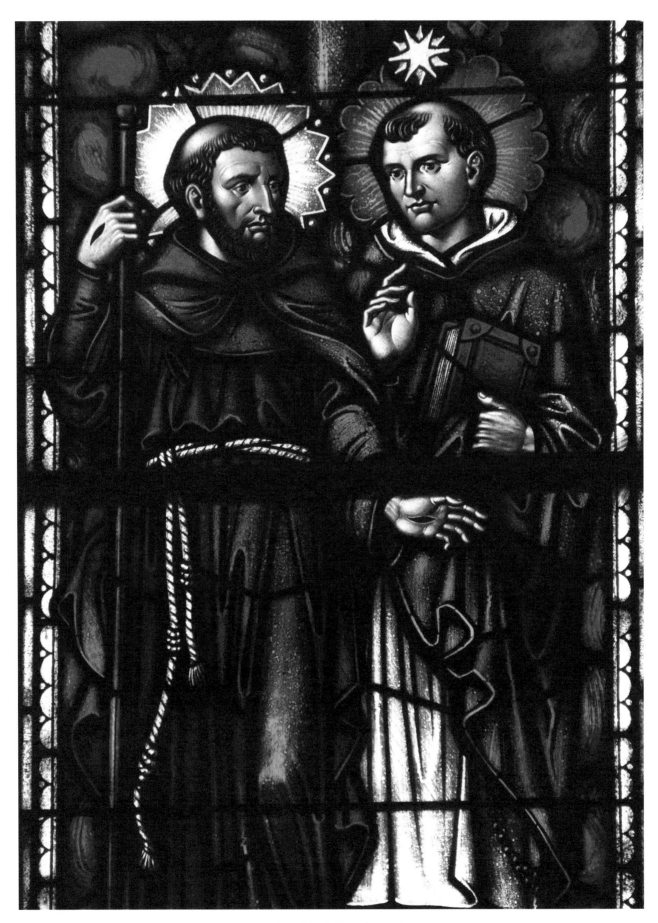

St. Francis of Assisi and St. Dominic

114

Writing Names and Titles

Trace and Copy.

Monsignor O'Riley

Mr. and Mrs. L. Wilson

Sister Mary Agnes

Father McLucas

St. Francis of Assisi

Pope John Paul II

18-3

Cities, States, and Countries

Trace and copy.

Cheyenne, Wyoming

Albany, New York

Rome, Italy

Washington, D.C.

Write your own city and state (province):

The interior of Brompton Oratory, London, England

The Leaning Tower of Pisa peeking out from behind Pisa Cathedral

118

Famous Places

Trace and copy.

Mount Rushmore

Yellowstone Park

Niagara Falls

Grand Canyon

The White House

Catholic University

Holidays and Holy Days

Trace and copy.

Christmas   Easter

Independence Day

Labor Day

Octave of the Nativity

Good Friday

Immaculate Conception

Trace and copy.

Be kind to young,

Be kind to old.

You'll find it's worth

much more than gold.

More Books of the Bible

Trace and copy.

New Testament Books:

The four Gospels:

St. Matthew, St. Mark,

St. Luke, and St. John

Some Epistles: St. Paul

St. James, St. Peter

God Made the Oceans

Trace and copy.

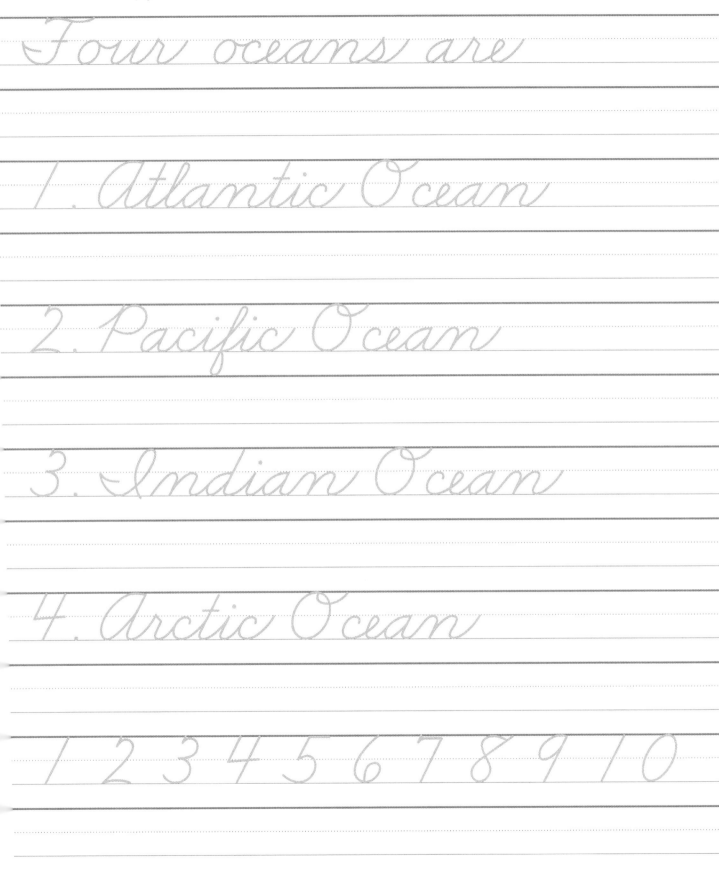

Four oceans are

1. Atlantic Ocean

2. Pacific Ocean

3. Indian Ocean

4. Arctic Ocean

1 2 3 4 5 6 7 8 9 10

God Made the Land

Trace and copy.

Seven Continents:

1. North America

2. South America

3. Europe   4. Asia

5. Africa   6. Australia

7. Antarctica

The Great Lakes

Trace and copy.

Five Great Lakes:

1. Huron

2. Ontario

3. Michigan

4. Erie

5. Superior

Santiago de Compostella, Spain

Some Countries in Europe

Trace and copy.

Portugal   Spain

Italy France Greece

Great Britain

Poland   Denmark

Holland   Ukraine

Russia   Ireland

Some Countries in Asia and Africa

Trace and copy.

Japan   Taiwan

Egypt   Israel

India   Thailand

Kenya   Philippines

South Korea   Turkey

Iran   Iraq

Some Countries of the Western Hemisphere

Trace and copy.

United States of America

Canada   Cuba   Mexico

Venezuela   Guatemala

Belize   El Salvador

Honduras   Nicaragua

Costa Rica   Panama

Planets of the Solar System

Trace and copy.

Mercury Venus Earth

Mars Jupiter Saturn

Uranus Neptune Pluto

The largest planet is

Jupiter.

The Creation of the Planets of the Solar System

Notre Dame Cathedral, Brussels, Belgium

Famous Cities of the World

Trace and copy.

New York Tokyo Cairo

Dublin Chicago Lima

Moscow Lisbon Paris

London Quebec Rome

Buenos Aires Brussels

New Delhi Sydney

Girls' Names

Trace and copy.

Agnes Barbara Clare

Grace Emily Felicity

Helen Isabel Xaviera

Jane Kateri Ruth Zita

Marie Olivia Dorothy

Sarah Theresa Ursula

Boys' Names

Trace and copy.

Dennis Fabian Giles

Hugh Isaac Andrew

Louis Martin Joseph

Pius Quentin Urban

Vincent Xavier Yves

William Zachary Eric

Days of the Week

Trace and copy.

Sunday

Monday

Tuesday

Wednesday

Thursday

Friday

Saturday

Fill in the blanks.

We must attend Mass

every _____.

Jesus died on the Cross

on Good _____.

22-3

Months of the Year

Trace and copy.

January

February

March

April

May

June

July

August

September

October

November

December

The Assumption

Calendar Clues

Write the month in which each holiday or holy day occurs.

All Souls Day

Independence Day

Assumption Day

Father's Day

Mother's Day

Choose from these months to complete your answer.

June, July August, November, May

23-1

Can You Name the Saint?

Write which saint is the patron of each. Choose from the box.

St. Joseph, St. Isidore the Farmer, St. Blaise, St. Jude,
St. Anthony, St. Nicholas, St. Lucy, St. Christopher,
The Holy Family, St. Luke

lost articles

children

eyes

hopeless cases

doctors

farmers

travel

sore throats

fathers

families

St. Anthony of Padua and the Starving Donkey

Holy Matrimony

142

The Seven Sacraments

Trace and copy.

Baptism

Confirmation

Holy Eucharist

Penance

Anointing of the Sick

Holy Orders

Matrimony

Underline the sacraments you have received.
Circle the sacrament you are preparing to receive.

23-3

The Gifts of the Holy Spirit

Trace and copy.

Wisdom

Understanding

Counsel

Fortitude

Knowledge

Piety

Fear of the Lord

There are seven gifts

of the Holy Spirit.

About Me

Using your best cursive handwriting,
give the information that tells about you and your family.

My name is

Mother's name:

Father's name:

Sister's name:

Brother's name:

Pet's name is

My city:

My state:

I live in the U.S. of _____

Parish church:

Letter Spacing

Correct spacing makes your writing easier to read. Trace and copy.

Correct spacing makes

writing easy to read.

easy to read

Do your best.

Write correctly.

Write the right way.

Foreign Languages

The Holy Father, the pope, travels to many countries throughout the world. Wherever he goes, he speaks to the people in their native tongue. Here are some of the languages that the Holy Father may have to speak. Trace and copy.

Latin Italian

French Spanish

Portuguese Russian

The Holy Father speaks

many languages.

I speak _____

On Your Own

You've had practice copying and writing cursive.
Now write each of these in your best cursive.

Abraham Lincoln

George Washington

John Quincy Adams

Thomas Jefferson

James Madison

These men were
American

James Madison

Solomon and Moses

Bible Heroes and Heroines

Trace and copy.

Moses

Esther

Raphael

Tobias

Sara

Naomi

Ruth

David

Solomon

Daniel

Noe

Judith

25-1

Modern-Day Heroes and Heroines

Trace and copy.

St. Maximillian Kolbe

St. Edith Stein

St. (Padre) Pio

Pope Francis

Write a sentence telling who your favorite hero is.

Favorite Sports

Trace and copy.

soccer tennis football

baseball   basketball

hockey   ice-skating

bicycling   swimming

bowling   ping-pong

golf   track and field

153

Favorite Musicians

Trace and copy.

Wolfgang A. Mozart

J. S. Bach   *Vivaldi*

Ludwig van Beethoven

Palestrina wrote

many beautiful

hymns for Holy Mass

Bible Verses

Copy this Bible verse below using your best cursive writing.

"In the beginning

was the Word, and

the Word was with

God, and the Word

was God." John 1:1

Jesus Christ is the Word.

More Bible Verses

Copy this Bible verse below using your best cursive writing.

"And now there
remain Faith, Hope,
and Charity, these
three: but the greatest
of these is Charity."
I Corinthians 13:13

The Good Samaritan shows charity.

Uppercase Letter Review

Trace and copy.

a

Anselm   Anne

Arthur Asia Alabama

Africa Alice Arkansas

Athanasius Anthony

Adam was in

Alaska in August.

Trace and copy.

C

Catholic Catechism

Canada California

Claire Confirmation

Communion Christ

Christ founded the

Catholic Church.

Trace and copy.

O

Ontario Oregon

Oscar Olivia Otto

Oklahoma Ohio

The Oregon Trail

Original Sin comes

from Adam and Eve.

Trace and copy.

E

English Easter

Epiphany Edmund

El Paso Evanston

Epistle Ephesians Eve

Queen Esther saved

her people.

Trace and copy.

m

Montana Missoula

Missouri May March

Mary Magdalen Maria

Martha Matthew Mark

Mary and Martha

loved Jesus.

Trace and copy.

n

Nativity Nicholas

Navajo Norfolk Newton

Newark Nebraska

Nantucket Nicene

Nina and Ned live

in Nevada.

Trace and copy.

Holy Hour Heaven

Hell Helena Honolulu

Halifax Hawaii Haiti

Henry Herman Hope

Honesty is the best

policy.

The Adoration of the Kings

Trace and copy.

K

Kerry Korea Kateri

Kenneth Karen King

Kyrie Eleison Katrina

"Kyrie Eleison" are words

in the Mass, meaning

"Lord, have mercy."

St. Valentine baptizing St. Lucilla

167

Trace and copy.

V

Valentine Vatican

Virginia Vermont

Vancouver Venezuela

Venerable Veritas

The Blessed Virgin

will help.

Trace and copy.

U

Uranus Utah Utica

United States Ukraine

Unction Urban Ursula

Uganda Uruguay

Blessed Urban V died

in 1370.

Trace and copy.

Y

Yakima Yorktown

Yukon Territory Yule

St. Yves Yonkers Yale

Yokohama Yemen

St. William of York,

pray for us!

Trace and copy.

Z

Zacharias St. Zita

Simon the Zealot

Zion Zacchaeus Zurich

Zambia Zanzibar Zulu

Zacharias was a

prophet.

Trace and copy.

W

Wichita Wisconsin

White Plains Walter

Whitsunday Wasilla

Walt Whitman and

William Wordsworth

were poets.

X

Xavierian Xanthe

Francis Xavier Xerxes

Xenia, Ohio Xanadu

Xanthus Xanthippe

The Xingu River is

in Brazil.

Trace and copy.

T

Tennessee Texas

Taiwan Trinidad

Thomas Timothy

Mark Twain Topeka

The Holy Trinity is

a mystery.

Trace and copy.

F

Franciscan Feast

Florida Flagstaff

Holy Father Faust

First Friday Francis

Who are the Fourteen

Holy Helpers?

175

St. Francis

Trace and copy.

J

Jesuit Jeremias

Jericho Japan Joplin

Joseph was the foster

father of Jesus.

Little Jacinta saw

Our Lady.

Trace and copy.

I

Italy Indiana

Irene Iwo Jima

St. Ignatius Isaiah

Idaho Illinois Iowa

Farmers pray to St.

Isidore.

Trace and copy.

Q

QuoVadis   Qatar

Queenship   Quaker

Queen of Heaven

Quebec   St. Quentin

Our Lady appeared at

Quito, Equador.

Trace and copy.

S

Sacred Heart

Abraham and Sara

Santa Fe   Sicily

Blessed Junipero Serra

began missions in

California.

St. George

Trace and copy.

G

Georgia Grenada

Guam St. Germaine

St. Gregory Grenoble

St. Gemma Galgani

St. George is the

patron of England.

Trace and copy.

D

Delaware Dallas

Denver Detroit

Divine Praises

Deuteronomy David

Daniel was cast into

the lions' den.

Trace and copy.

L

Louisiana Lee

Lexington Louisville

Love of God

Love of neighbor

Remember, keep holy

the Lord's Day.

Trace and copy.

P

Pennsylvania

Pope Paul   Marco Polo

Peter's Pence   Passion

Polycarp   Paschal

Palm Sunday begins

Holy Week.

Trace and copy.

R *R*

Resurrection

Roman Rite   Regina

Paul Revere   Reverend

Rachel and Jacob

Rebecca was the mother

of Jacob and Esau.

Trace and copy.

B

Byzantine

Beatitude   Baptism

Blessed Sacrament

Body and Blood

Jesus gave us the

eight Beatitudes.

Number Practice

Trace and copy.

1 1 1 1 1 2 2 2 2 2

3 3 3 3 3 4 4 4 4 4

5 5 5 5 5 6 6 6 6 6

7 7 7 7 7 8 8 8 8 8

9 9 9 9 9 10 10 10 10 10

1 2 3 4 5 6 7 8 9 10

Know Your Numbers

Trace and copy.

one 1 two 2

three 3 four 4

five 5 six 6

seven 7 eight 8

nine 9 ten 10

Go back and mark with a dot the starting point of each number.
Write your street address below.

The Ten Commandments

Mary and Jesus

Trace and copy.

Jesus and Mary want
me to do my very
best. I will always
try to work neatly
and use my best
cursive writing.

A Night Prayer

Trace and copy.

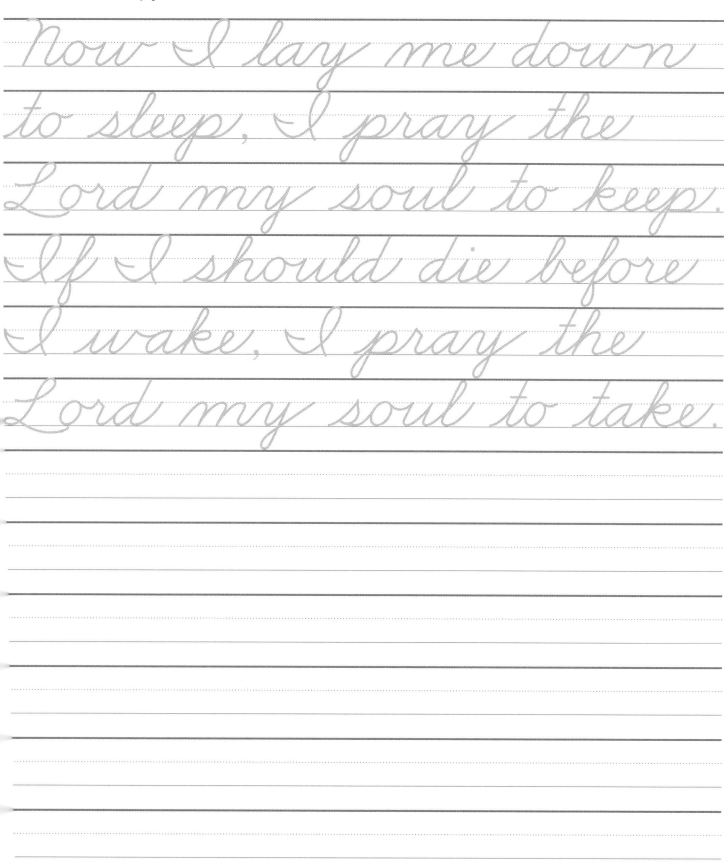

Now I lay me down to sleep, I pray the Lord my soul to keep. If I should die before I wake, I pray the Lord my soul to take.

193

The Thing to Do
by Mary Dixon Thayer

Trace.

To please you, God,

I know that I

Need not do any

Thing but try

To be as good

As I can be

Because You lived

And died for me.

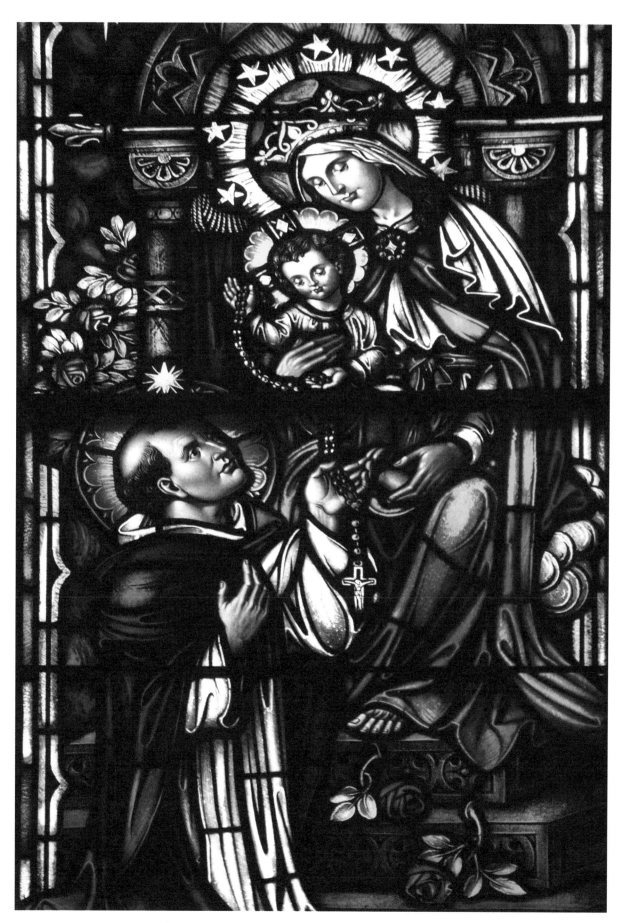

St. Dominic receives the Rosary from Our Lady.

195

F is for Father
by Hilda van Stockum

Write over the shaded letters of this poem.

God created stars and

storms

And orchards and the

sea;

He reigns above the

golden clouds

In endless majesty.

And yet the little child

Who toddles here below

May say "Our

Father" to this King,

For Jesus taught us so

31-4

196

Copy the poem from the previous page.

Days of the Week

Write the days of the week in the correct order.
The first one is done for you.

> *Wednesday, Friday, Monday, Sunday*
> *Tuesday, Saturday, Thursday*

1. Sunday
2.
3.
4.
5.
6.
7.

We go to Mass

on _____.

Months of the Year

Write the months of the year in the correct order.
The first one is done for you.

> *September, February, June, October, January, May*
> *August, March, November, July, December, April*

1. January
2.
3.
4.
5.
6.

7.
8.
9.
10.
11.
12.

Christmas is
in _____.

Spring begins
in _____.

The Liturgical Year

Trace and copy.

Liturgical Year

Advent

Christmas

Lent

Easter

Pentecost

The holy season of

Lent lasts forty days.

St. Albert the Great

Writing a Friendly Letter

May 6, 2014

Dear Joey,

My dog Spanky just had five puppies! They are white with brown spots and are the cutest little beagles I've ever seen. I'd like you to have one. Please come and see them soon.

Your cousin,

Billy

Copy the letter from the previous page.

St. Joan of Arc

Abbreviations

Trace and copy.

Mr. Mrs. Dr. St.

Fr. Sr. Rev. S.J.

Mrs. William Turner

Fr. John Hardon, S.J.

Sr. Mary Agnes

St. Isabel of France

Contractions

Trace and copy.

I'm I'll I'd isn't

didn't won't can't

haven't couldn't

wouldn't shouldn't

I will I won't

I do I don't

Capital Letters in Book Titles

Trace and copy.

Good St. Joseph

Black Beauty

Bambi   King Arthur

Robin Hood   Cinderella

Joan of Arc

Thumbelina   Heidi

Somersault
by Dorothy Aldis

Trace, then copy this poem on the next page.

I somersault just
like a clown,
And all the trees
turn upside down.
The sky is not the
sky at all.
It changes to a high
blue wall,
And every little
buttercup
Looks down at me
instead of up.

34-1

Use your best cursive to copy the poem.

Fourth of July Night
by Dorothy Aldis

Trace this poem.

Pinwheels whirling
round
Spit sparks upon the
ground,
And rockets shoot up
high
And blossom in the
sky.

Blue and yellow, green
and red,
Flowers falling on
my head,
I never have to go to
bed,
Down to bed, to bed,
to bed!

St. Hyacinth, the Apostle of Poland, bravely rescued the statue of Our Lady.

Joining Letters

Trace and copy.

bb bl be br by bv

babble obvious baby

ve va vo vy vir vv

Navy survive twelve

wh wa we wi wo

own what away will

Joining Letters

Trace and copy.

ya by yo ye tty li

hymn jetty quilt

xi ox xy xc ex xt xe

taxi oxen proxy except

mpt ma mm mn

empty teammate

Joining Letters

Trace and copy.

ui ur un wu vu

built fur sunny quiet

oi io oa oe oo ou

toil Pio boat foe school

zy zz gz oz az zi

dizzy zigzag dozen gaze

Joining Letters

Trace and copy.

yp ga eg gs go ng

eggs Egypt game going

ja je ju nj jo jy ji

jail jest just enjoy

ka ck nk ke ki ky

kangaroo clock sink

Joining Letters

Trace and copy.

pa pp py pu sp pt

puppy split pal

qu sq cq iq uqu eq

quail square acquire

ca cc ck sc cr cu oc

cart occur sick crush

St. Cecilia

Joining Uppercase Letters

Trace and copy.

Ad At Al Am Ar Ac

Adam Alaska Amy

Ba Bu Bl Bo Bu Br

Back Bob Brooklyn

Ca Cr Cu Ce Cl Co Ch Ci

Cape Cod Cecilia China

Joining Uppercase Letters

Trace and copy.

Da Di Dry Do

Ea Ev Eg Ed Edward

Ft Fr Fa Fl Ft

Ga Gl Go Gr Gloria

Ha He Hu Ho Huron

Io Il Im It Iowa

Joining Uppercase Letters

Trace and copy.

Ja Je Jo Ju Jane Jill

Ka Kr Ke Kn Karl

La Lu Lo Le Luke

Mr Mi Ma Mr. Mrs.

Ni Na Nu Ne Niagara

Ol Or Om Ot Olga

Joining Uppercase Letters

Trace and copy.

Pa Pi Pl Pr Bl.

Qu Qua Que Quebec

Ri Ra Ru Racine

Sa So St Su

Tr Th To Thomas

Toledo Utah Uruguay

Joining Uppercase Letters

Trace and copy.

Va Ve Vo Venice Vincent

Wh Wa Wo World War

Xe Xy Xa Xenia Ohio

Ya Yu Ye Youngstown

Za Ze Zu Zambia Zita

Jerusalem Kansas City

Appendix

Review of Manuscript Letters

Touch the dot on the headline; slant left to the dot on the baseline; lift. Touch the dot on the headline; slant right to the dot on the baseline; lift. Touch the dot on the midline; slide right to the dot. Lift.

Touch the dot below the midline; circle back counterclockwise all the way around. Push up straight to the dot on the midline. Pause; pull down straight to the dot on the baseline. Lift.

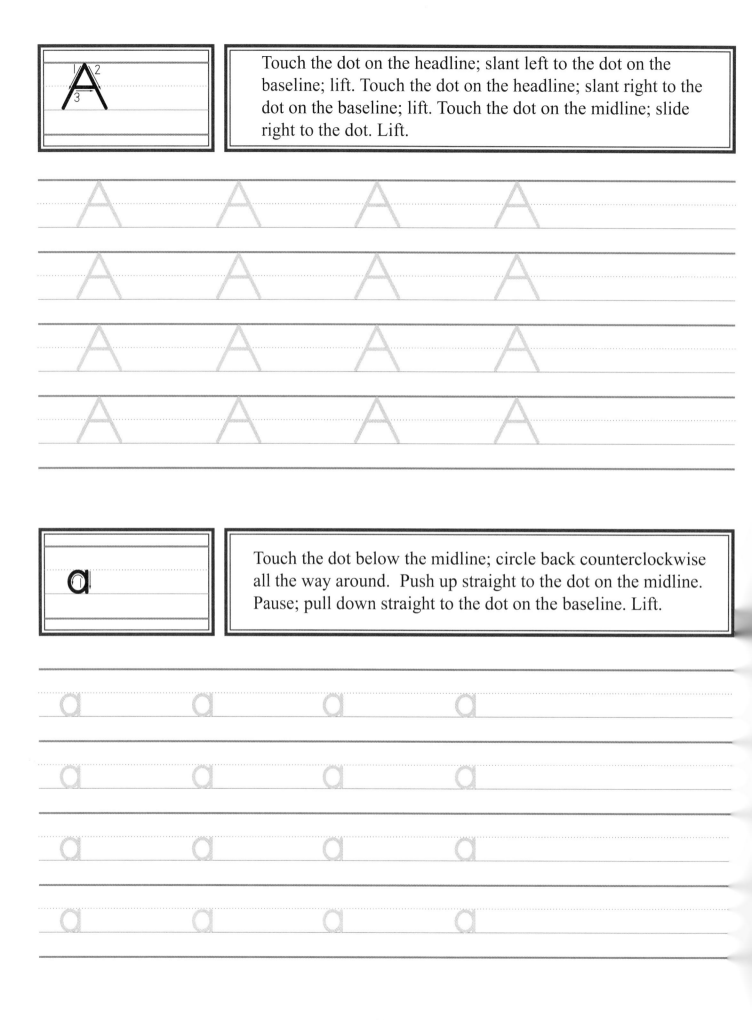

Touch the dot on the headline; pull down straight to the dot on the baseline. Lift. Touch the dot on the headline; slide right; curve forward right to the midline; slide left to the dot. Pause; slide right; curve forward right to the baseline. Slide left to the dot. Lift.

Touch the dot on the headline; pull down straight to the dot on the baseline. Pause; push up; circle forward clockwise all the way around. Lift.

C

Touch the dot below the headline; circle back counterclockwise, touching the headline, midline, and baseline, and ending on the dot above the baseline. Lift.

C   C   C   C

C   C   C   C

C   C   C   C

C   C   C   C

C

Touch the dot below the midline; circle back counterclockwise, touching the midline, and the baseline, and ending on the dot above the baseline. Lift.

c   c   c   c

c   c   c   c

c   c   c   c

c   c   c   c

228

Touch the dot on the headline; pull down straight to the dot on the baseline. Lift. Touch the dot on the headline; slide right; curve forward clockwise; slide left to the dot on the baseline. Lift.

D D D D

D D D D

D D D D

D D D D

Touch the dot below the midline; circle back counterclockwise all the way around. Push up straight to the dot on the headline. Pause; pull down straight to the dot on the baseline. Lift.

d d d d

d d d d

d d d d

d d d d

Touch the dot on the headline; pull down straight to the dot on the baseline. Lift. Touch the dot on the headline; slide right. Lift. Touch the dot on the midline; slide right. Stop short on the dot; Lift. Touch the dot on the baseline; slide right. Lift.

Touch the dot halfway between the midline and baseline; slide right to the dot; circle back counterclockwise, touching the midline, and the baseline, and ending on the dot above the baseline. Lift.

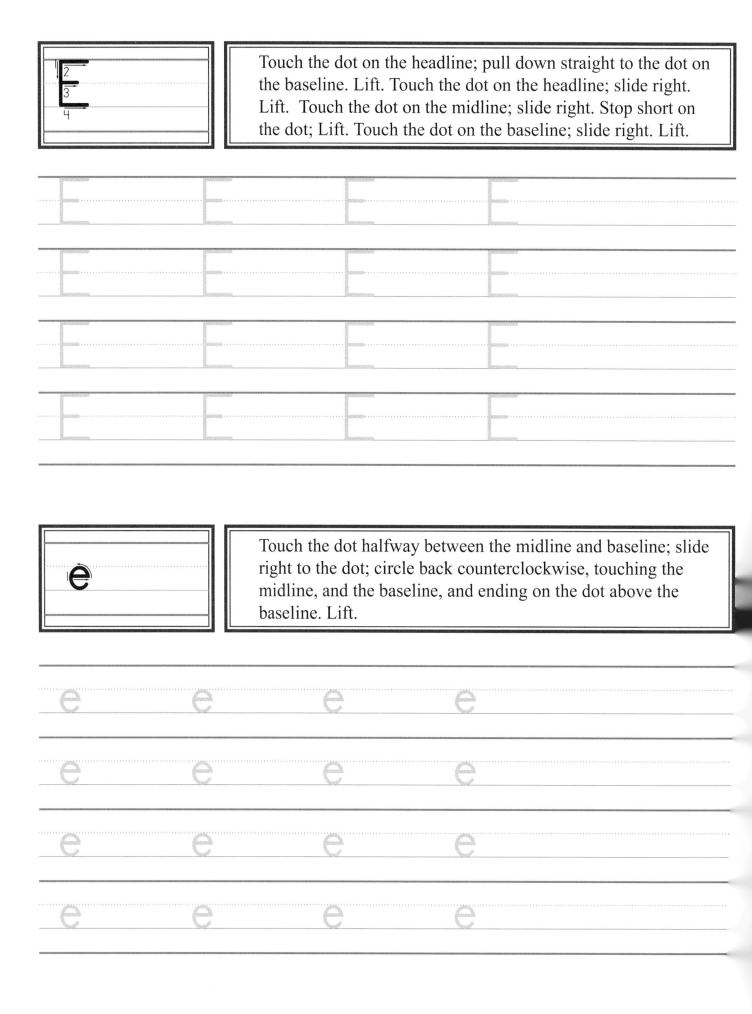

Touch the dot on the headline; pull down straight to the dot on the baseline. Lift. Touch the dot on the headline; slide right to the dot. Lift. Touch the dot on the midline; slide right. Stop short on the dot. Lift.

Touch the dot below the headline; curve back left; pull down straight to the dot on the baseline. Lift. Touch the dot on the midline; slide right to the dot. Lift.

G

Touch the dot below the headline; circle back counterclockwise, touching the headline, midline, and baseline, and ending on the dot on the midline; slide left to the dot. Lift.

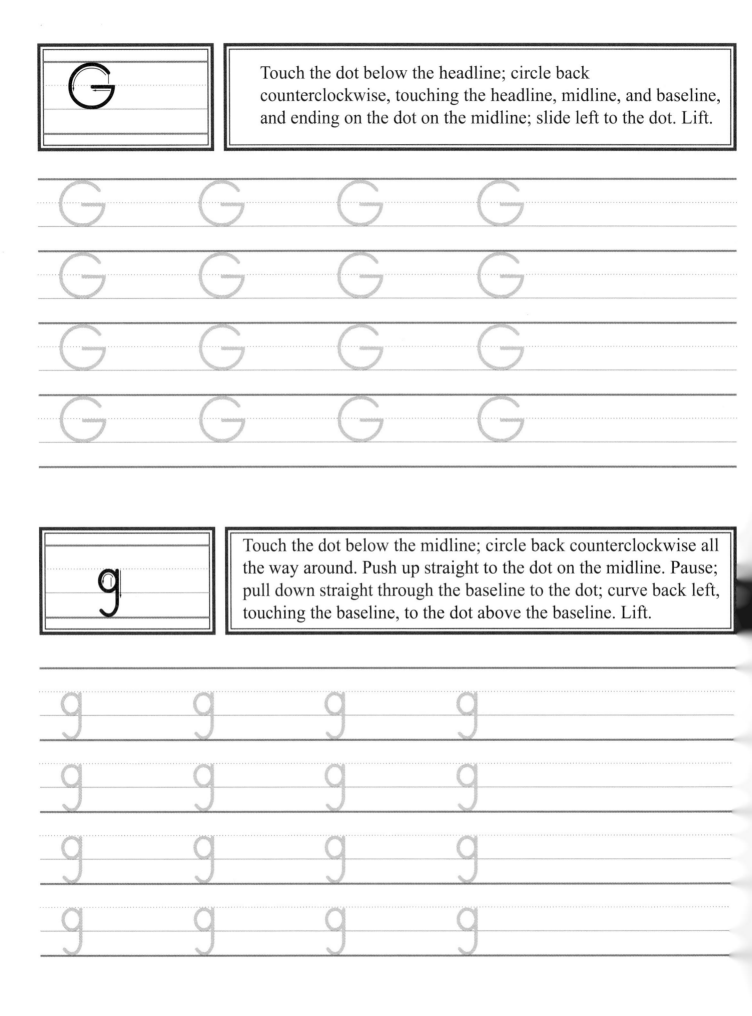

g

Touch the dot below the midline; circle back counterclockwise all the way around. Push up straight to the dot on the midline. Pause; pull down straight through the baseline to the dot; curve back left, touching the baseline, to the dot above the baseline. Lift.

Touch the dot on the headline; pull down straight to the dot on the baseline. Lift. Touch the dot on the headline; pull down straight to the dot on the baseline. Lift. Move to the left and touch the dot on the midline; slide right to the dot. Lift.

Touch the dot on the headline; pull down straight to the dot on the baseline. Pause; push up; curve forward right; pull down straight to the dot on the baseline. Lift.

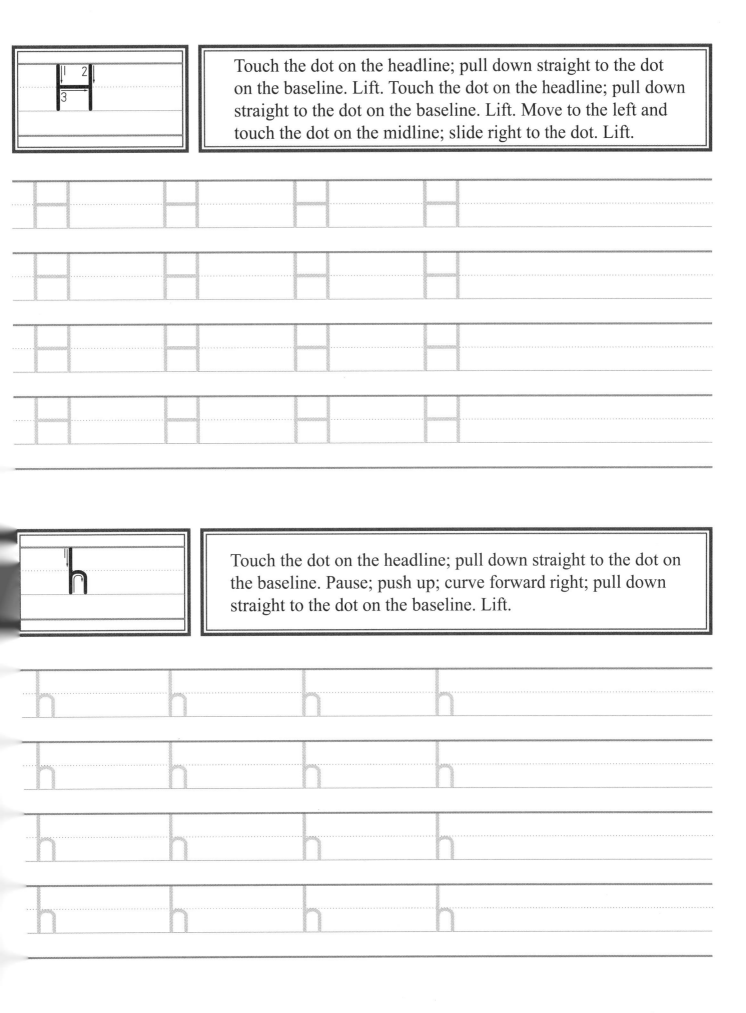

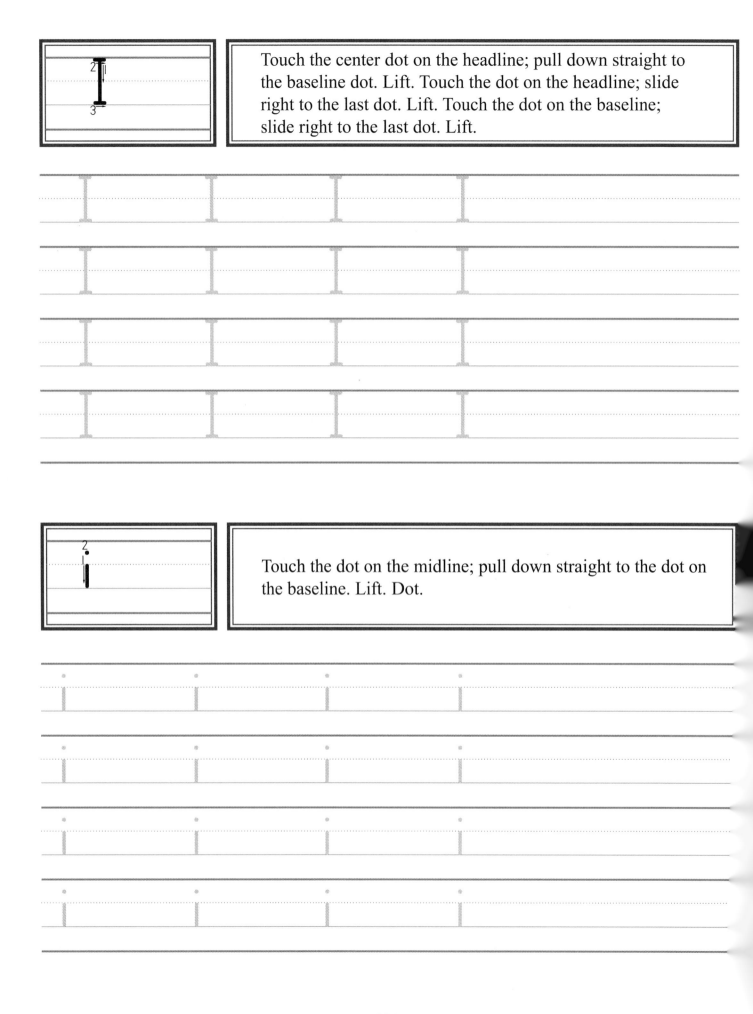

Touch the center dot on the headline; pull down straight to the baseline dot. Lift. Touch the dot on the headline; slide right to the last dot. Lift. Touch the dot on the baseline; slide right to the last dot. Lift.

Touch the dot on the midline; pull down straight to the dot on the baseline. Lift. Dot.

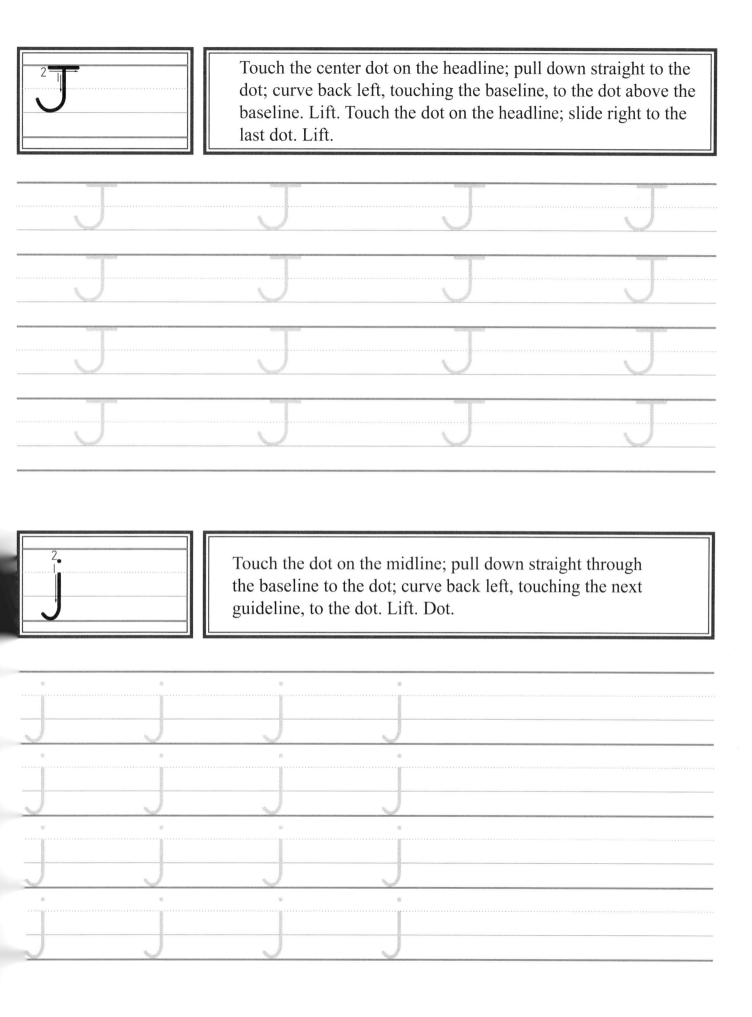

Touch the center dot on the headline; pull down straight to the dot; curve back left, touching the baseline, to the dot above the baseline. Lift. Touch the dot on the headline; slide right to the last dot. Lift.

Touch the dot on the midline; pull down straight through the baseline to the dot; curve back left, touching the next guideline, to the dot. Lift. Dot.

235

K

Touch the dot on the headline; pull down straight to the dot on the baseline. Lift. Move to the right and touch the dot on the headline; slant left to the dot on the midline. Pause; slant right to the dot on the baseline. Lift.

K   K   K   K

K   K   K   K

K   K   K   K

K   K   K   K

k

Touch the dot on the headline; pull down straight to the dot on the baseline. Lift. Move to the right and touch the dot on the midline; slant left to the dot. Pause; slant right to the dot on the baseline. Lift.

k   k   k   k

k   k   k   k

k   k   k   k

k   k   k   k

Touch the dot on the headline; pull down straight to the dot on the baseline. Pause; slide right to the dot. Lift.

Touch the dot on the headline; pull down straight to the dot on the baseline. Lift.

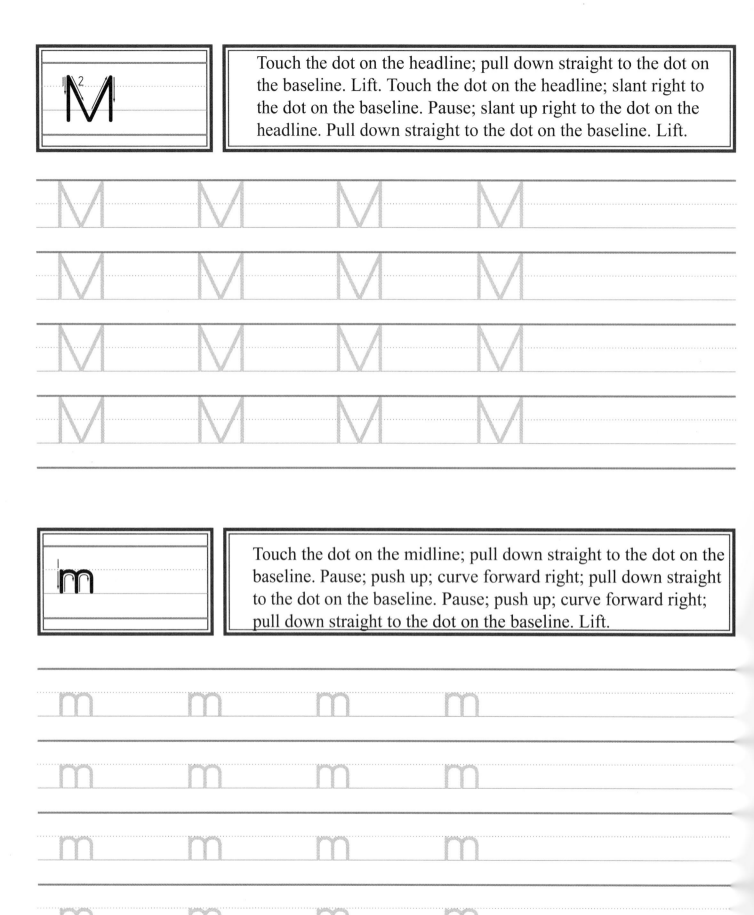

Touch the dot on the headline; pull down straight to the dot on the baseline. Lift. Touch the dot on the headline; slant right to the dot on the baseline. Pause; slant up right to the dot on the headline. Pull down straight to the dot on the baseline. Lift.

Touch the dot on the midline; pull down straight to the dot on the baseline. Pause; push up; curve forward right; pull down straight to the dot on the baseline. Pause; push up; curve forward right; pull down straight to the dot on the baseline. Lift.

N

Touch the dot on the headline; pull down straight to the dot on the baseline. Lift.
Touch the dot on the headline; slant right to the dot on the baseline. Pause; push up straight to the dot on the headline. Lift.

N   N   N   N

N   N   N   N

N   N   N   N

N   N   N   N

n

Touch the dot on the midline; pull down straight to the dot on the baseline. Pause; push up; curve forward right, touching the midline; pull down straight to the dot on the baseline. Lift.

n   n   n   n

n   n   n   n

n   n   n   n

n   n   n   n

Touch the dot below the headline; circle back counterclockwise, back to the same dot. Lift.

Touch the dot below the midline; circle back counterclockwise, back to the same dot. Lift.

Touch the dot on the headline; pull down straight to the dot on the baseline. Lift.
Touch the dot on the headline; slide right; curve forward right to the midline; slide left to the dot on the midline. Lift.

Touch the dot on the midline; pull down straight through the baseline to the dot on the next guideline. Pause; push up; curve forward clockwise all the way around to the dot above the baseline. Lift.

Touch the dot below the headline; circle back counterclockwise, back to the same dot. Lift. Touch the dot between the midline and baseline; slant right to the dot on the baseline. Lift.

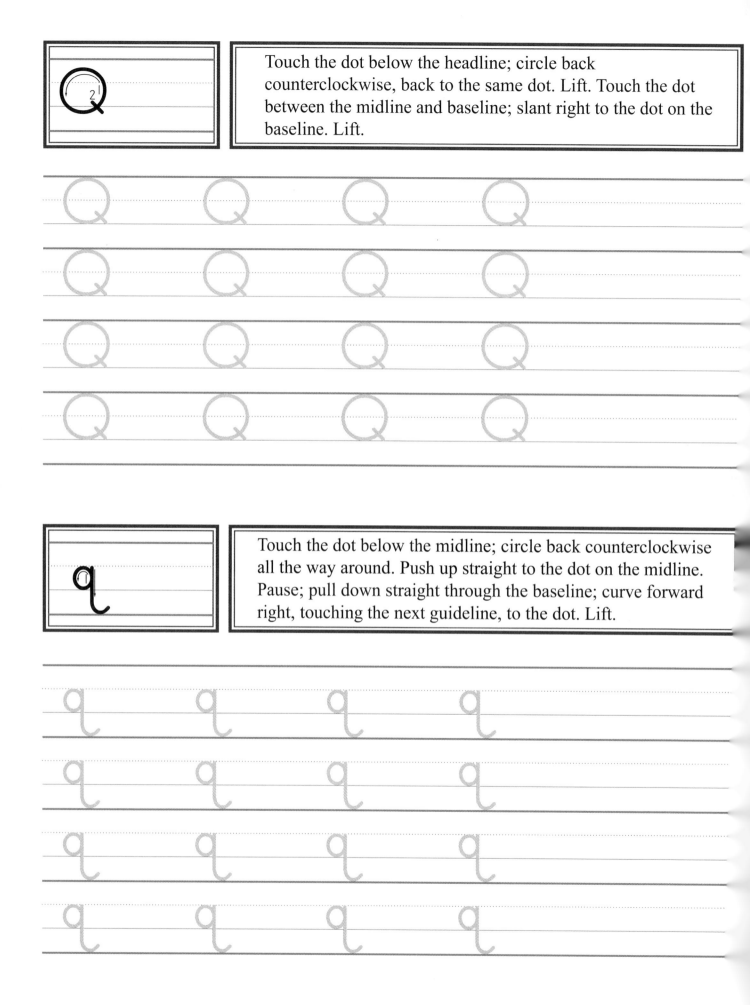

Touch the dot below the midline; circle back counterclockwise all the way around. Push up straight to the dot on the midline. Pause; pull down straight through the baseline; curve forward right, touching the next guideline, to the dot. Lift.

Touch the dot on the headline; pull down straight to the dot on the baseline. Lift. Touch the dot on the headline; slide right; curve forward right to the midline; slide left to the dot on the midline. Pause; slant right to the dot on the baseline. Lift.

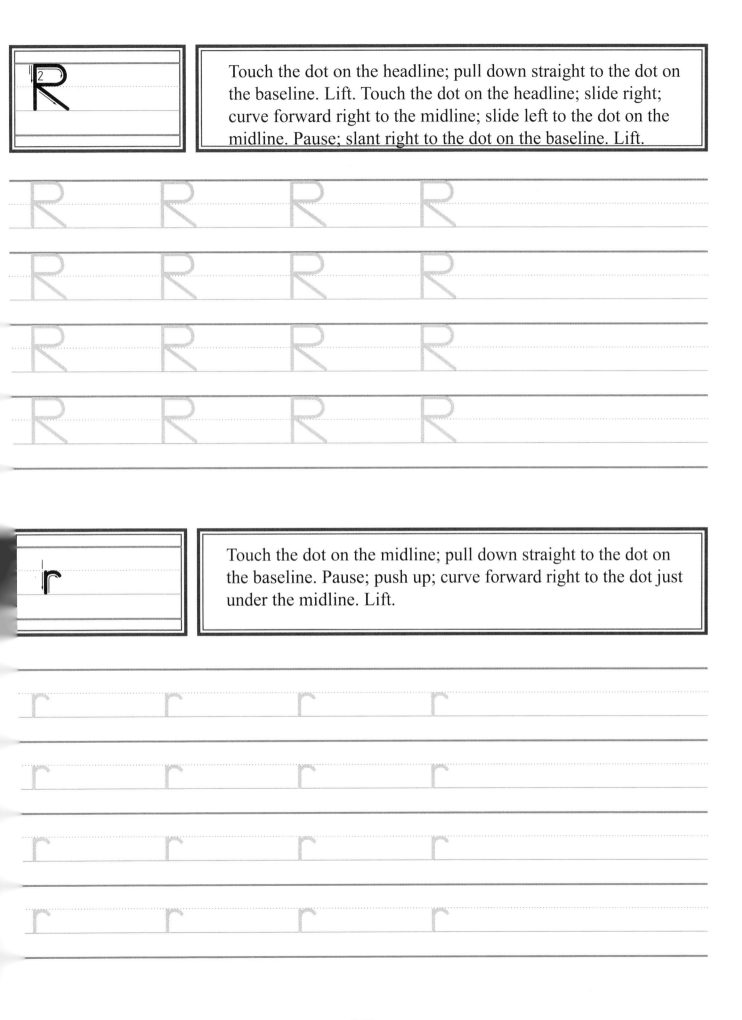

Touch the dot on the midline; pull down straight to the dot on the baseline. Pause; push up; curve forward right to the dot just under the midline. Lift.

S

Touch the dot below the headline; curve back left; curve forward right, ending on the dot just above the baseline. Lift.

S   S   S   S

S   S   S   S

S   S   S   S

S   S   S   S

s

Touch the dot below the midline; curve back left; curve forward right, ending on the dot just above the baseline. Lift.

s   s   s   s

s   s   s   s

s   s   s   s

s   s   s   s

244

Touch the center dot on the headline; pull down straight to the dot on the baseline. Lift. Touch the left dot on the headline; slide right to the last dot. Lift.

Touch the dot on the headline; pull down straight to the dot on the baseline. Lift. Touch the dot on the midline; slide right to the dot. Lift.

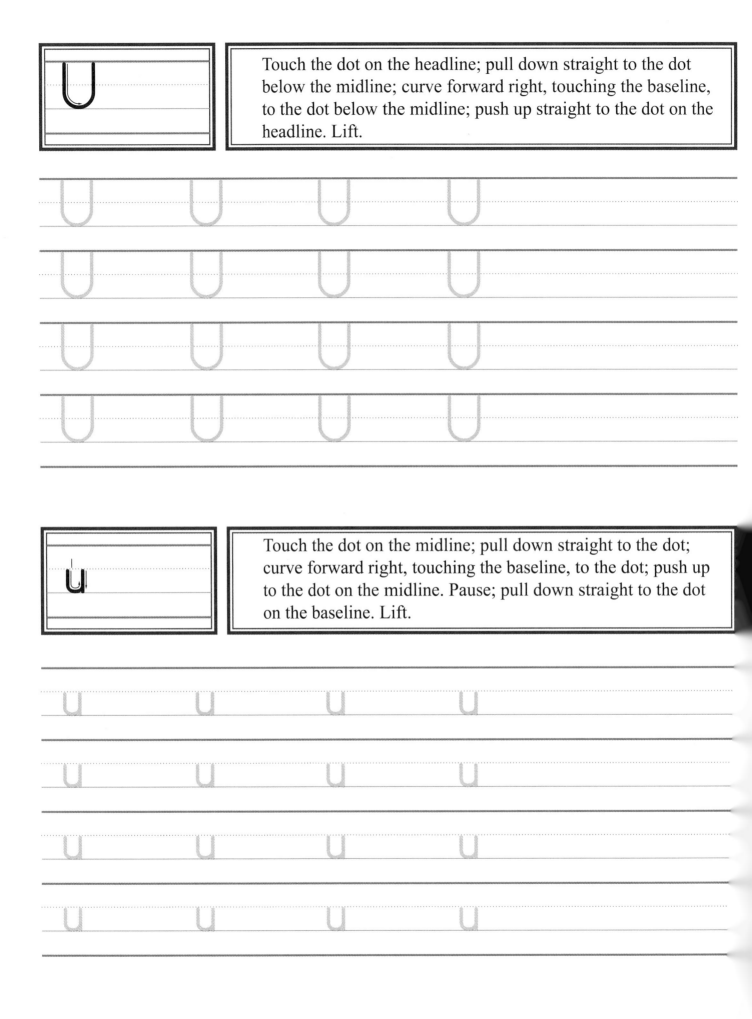

Touch the dot on the headline; pull down straight to the dot below the midline; curve forward right, touching the baseline, to the dot below the midline; push up straight to the dot on the headline. Lift.

Touch the dot on the midline; pull down straight to the dot; curve forward right, touching the baseline, to the dot; push up to the dot on the midline. Pause; pull down straight to the dot on the baseline. Lift.

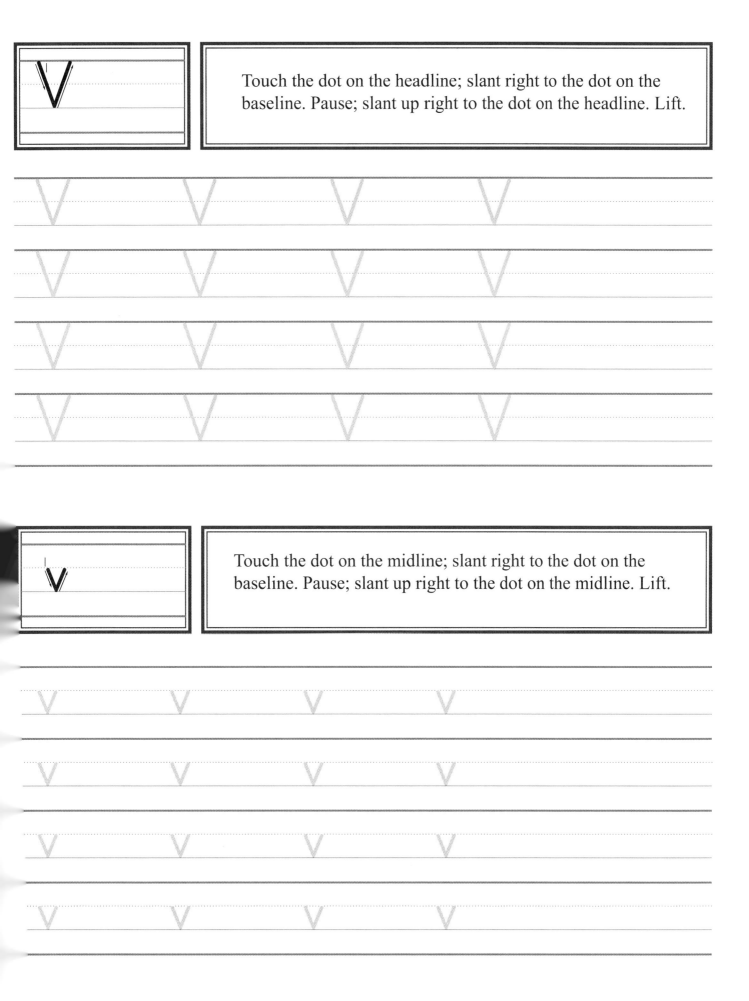

Touch the dot on the headline; slant right to the dot on the baseline. Pause; slant up right to the dot on the headline. Lift.

Touch the dot on the midline; slant right to the dot on the baseline. Pause; slant up right to the dot on the midline. Lift.

247

W

Touch the dot on the headline; slant right to the dot on the baseline. Pause; slant up right to the dot on the headline. Pause; slant right to the dot on the baseline. Pause; slant up right to the dot on the headline. Lift.

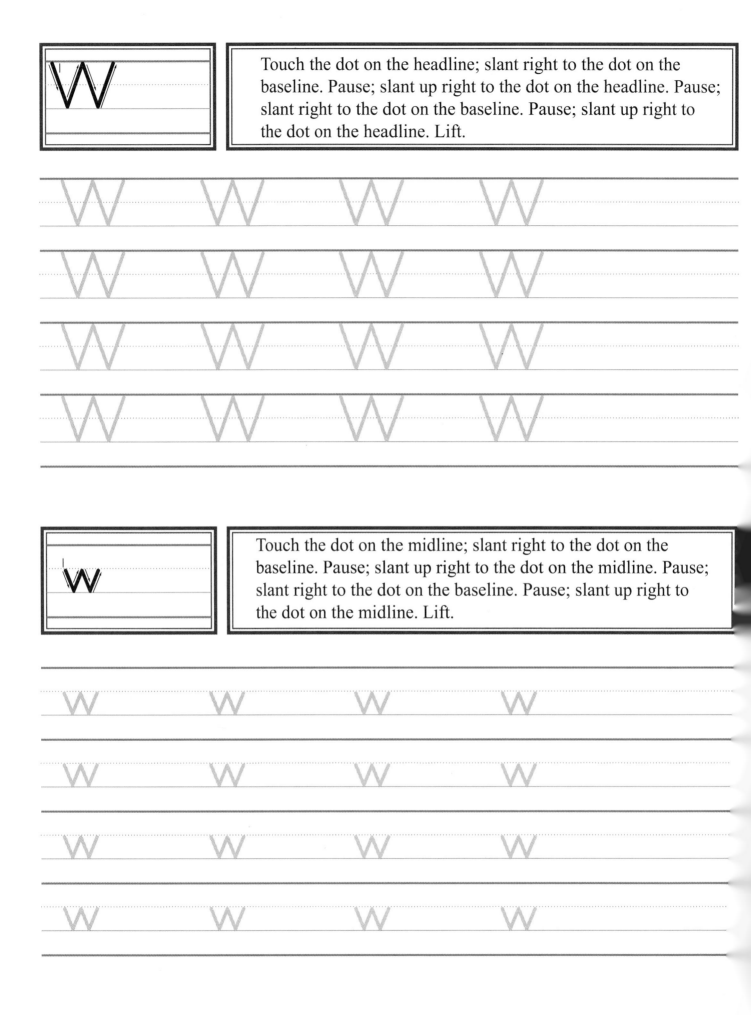

w

Touch the dot on the midline; slant right to the dot on the baseline. Pause; slant up right to the dot on the midline. Pause; slant right to the dot on the baseline. Pause; slant up right to the dot on the midline. Lift.

Touch the dot on the headline; slant right to the dot on the baseline. Lift. Move to the right and touch the dot on the headline; slant left to the dot on the baseline, crossing near the midline. Lift.

Touch the dot on the midline; slant right to the dot on the baseline. Lift. Move to the right and touch the dot on the midline; slant left to the dot on the baseline. Lift.

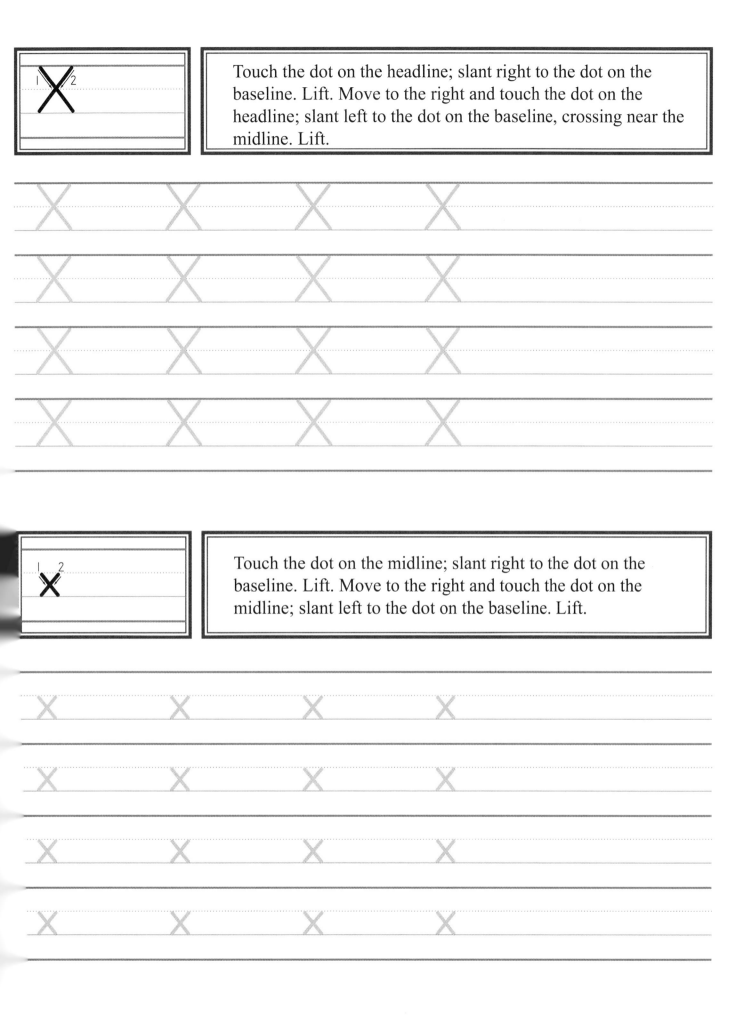

Touch the dot on the headline; slant right to the dot on the midline. Lift. Move to the right and touch the dot on the headline; slant left to the dot on the midline. Pull down straight to the dot on the baseline. Lift.

Y Y Y Y

Y Y Y Y

Y Y Y Y

Y Y Y Y

Touch the dot on the midline; slant right to the dot on the baseline. Lift. Move to the right and touch the dot on the midline; slant left through the dot on the baseline, to the dot on the next line. Lift.

y y y y

y y y y

y y y y

y y y y

Touch the dot on the headline; slide right to the dot. Pause; slant left to the dot on the baseline. Pause; slide right to the dot. Lift.

Touch the dot on the midline; slide right to the dot. Pause; slant left to the dot on the baseline. Pause; slide right to the dot. Lift.

Touch the dot on the headline. Pull down straight to the dot on the baseline. Lift.

Touch the dot below the headline. Curve forward right; slant Left to the dot on the baseline. Slide right to the dot. Lift.

2 2 2 2

2 2 2 2

2 2 2 2

2 2 2 2

3

Touch the dot below the headline. Curve forward right to the dot on the midline; curve forward right ending at the dot above the baseline. Lift.

3   3   3   3

3   3   3   3

3   3   3   3

3   3   3   3

4

Touch the dot on the headline. Pull down straight to the dot on the midline; slide right to the dot. Lift. Touch the dot on the headline. Pull down straight to the dot on the baseline. Lift.

4   4   4   4

4   4   4   4

4   4   4   4

4   4   4   4

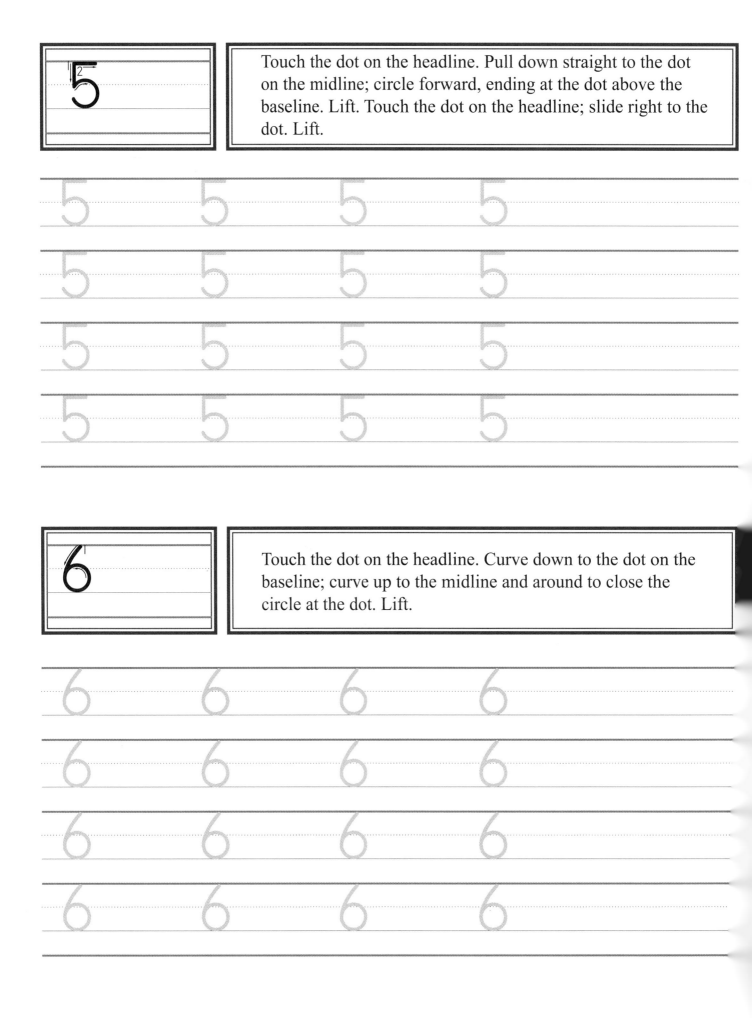

Touch the dot on the headline. Pull down straight to the dot on the midline; circle forward, ending at the dot above the baseline. Lift. Touch the dot on the headline; slide right to the dot. Lift.

Touch the dot on the headline. Curve down to the dot on the baseline; curve up to the midline and around to close the circle at the dot. Lift.

7

Touch the dot on the headline. Slide right to the dot; slant left to the dot on the baseline. Lift.

8

Touch the dot below the headline. Curve back left to the midline; curve forward right, touching the dot on the baseline and up to the midline; slant up right to the dot on the headline. Lift.

9

Touch the dot below the headline. Circle back all the way around to the same dot; pull straight down to the dot on the baseline. Lift.

9   9   9   9

9   9   9   9

9   9   9   9

9   9   9   9

10

Touch the dot on the headline. Pull straight down to the dot on the baseline. Lift. Touch the dot on the headline. Curve down to the dot on the baseline; curve up to the same dot on the headline. Lift.

10   10   10   10

10   10   10   10

10   10   10   10

10   10   10   10

Like our books?

You might like our program, too. Seton Home Study School offers a full curriculum program for Pre-Kindergarten through Twelfth Grade. We include daily lesson plans, answer keys, quarterly tests, and much more. Our staff of teachers and counselors is available to answer questions and offer help. We keep student records and send out diplomas that are backed by our accreditation with the Southern Association of Colleges and Schools and the AdvancEd Accreditation Commission.

For more information about Seton Home Study School,

please contact our admissions office.